PRAISE FOR *START LESS, FINISH MOR*

Dan has applied agile thinking and techniques to strategy in an elegar
His five-step process—assess, focus, commit, act, and learn—f
ing less and accomplishing more, all in alignment with the entu
analogy is quite apropos and hooked me right away. I highly
entertaining, and informative book. Well done Dan.

—JIM STOCKMAL, President, Association fo.   .ianning

It's not often you find a book that provides a complete yet simple approach to tackling
the most important challenges every organization must face and overcome to achieve
long-lasting success. *Start Less, Finish More* does just that. Dan Montgomery has built
upon the foundation of the powerful Balanced Scorecard system, adapted it for today's
turbulent times, and also convincingly shown how OKRs can be used to drive agility
and execution.

—PAUL NIVEN, author of *Balanced Scorecard Step by Step*
and *Objectives and Key Results*

This book is the real deal! That's exactly how I felt when I finished reading *Start Less,
Finish More*. In an interesting and practical way, Dan Montgomery used his pen to lay out
the rationale and process for incorporating strategic agility into the strategic management discipline. Unlike anything else I've read thus far, Dan does a great job of explain-
ing the intersection of strategic agility and human psychology. I especially appreciated
his ability to build on the proven foundations of strategic management while pointing out
the strategy execution challenges organizations face in our ever changing and sometimes
disrupted world.

—RANDALL ROLLINSON, President, LBL Strategies

Real advancements in strategy management do not come often. Dan has moved the
ball forward by collecting strategic planning, human-centered design, and agile delivery techniques from today's most successful tech companies and put them together into
a simple and innovative framework that is accessible to anyone.

—GABRIEL MORGAN, Enterprise Architect and Digital
Transformation Executive for Microsoft, Starbucks, and REI

Dan has codified many of the agile business practices that we experimented with at Rally. He is certainly more comprehensive, articulate, and coherent then we ever were. His effective linking of OKRs into overall practices is fantastic. I know that many businesses struggle with the right level and scope of OKRs, and Dan spells it out straight for you to execute and go. This is a super pragmatic book that is comprehensively researched and based on years of practice and consulting. I would call this approach state of the art.

———

A much needed take on how to work on strategy iteratively in high-speed agile organizations. Dan talks frankly about the failures of traditional strategic planning and then offers straightforward solutions to those problems. For Dan, strategy is a learning loop, and he gives clear guidance on how to run that loop with everyone in your organization. He also provides great examples from current companies that are finding new ways to learn quickly.

It is hard to prescribe an approach for working on strategy, because this work obviously has to be tailored to the specifics of an organization. But Dan manages to balance this. He starts with frameworks and then offers very specific guidance on how to think about who should meet and how often, as well as how many items you should plan at different levels.

This book will not magically make strategy easy or reduce the amount of strategy management work that is needed. What it can do is increase the impact of your strategic work. In the end, that's what matters to me.

———

For something so simple, OKRs are surprisingly hard to do right. In Dan's book, *Start Less, Finish More*, he takes this simple idea, shows you how hard it is really is, and then makes it simple again by showing you how to do it. By exploring corporate strategy, from ideation to execution, this book manages to be both insightful and practical.

———

When I learned to ride a bike, I had to get up and try several times before I understood how to launch, keep my balance, and pedal. There was far more to it than my never-ridden-a-bike-before mind could have fathomed. It wasn't until my body engaged in the process that I really understood how to do it. This is a universal truth that also applies to the business world. With *Start Less, Finish More*, Dan provides a practical guide for how to become a more effective organization by recognizing how we really get good at things. He provides a toolkit for those of us who actually have to deploy a strategy, not just think about it. Dan gives us a discipline to avoid getting bogged down in information overload or too many divergent projects, along with how to keep up the momentum of progress and how to get the most out of people. This is a guidebook for those who really want to improve results and ensure that their desired future becomes reality.

—CHRISTIAN KULAK, Strategic Planning Director,
Excellus Blue Cross Blue Shield, Rochester, NY

———

Dan Montgomery summarizes a twenty-year career in strategic planning with a practical step-by-step framework for creating and executing strategic plans in the face of today's fast-paced, complex markets. His method applies techniques originally developed in Silicon Valley to the needs of a wider range of organizations, from non-tech businesses to nonprofits and government agencies.

—ROD COLLINS, Director of Innovation, Optimity Advisors;
Innovation Sherpa, Salt Flats;
Author, *WikiManagement: A Revolutionary New Model
for a Rapidly Changing and Collaborative World*

———

Dan has created a practical approach to enable a more rapid cadence of strategy management appropriate for the ever-changing complexities of modern organizations. He builds on the strengths of the balanced scorecard and other best practices for strategic planning and performance management while integrating an agile execution method appropriate for the pace of change found in many organizations today. As a former colleague and coauthor of his, I appreciate Dan's clarity of thinking and how he approaches complex concepts to extract their most practical, understandable, and *useful* essence. This book is an essential for my reference library.

—GAIL STOUT PERRY, coauthor, *The Institute Way*,
Chief Strategy Officer and VP of Americas, Corporater

———

No one makes strategy accessible like Dan does.

—BRIAN CASSELL, DVM, Chief Strategy Officer
Ethos Veterinary Health

START LESS, **FINISH MORE**

START LESS
FINISH MORE

Building Strategic Agility
with Objectives and Key Results

DAN MONTGOMERY

Agile
Strategies
PRESS

Boulder, Colorado

ISBN: 978-1-7325397-0-9 (paperback)
ISBN: 978-1-7325397-1-6 (e-book)
LCCN: 2018909215

Published by Agile Strategies Press
2525 Arapahoe Avenue
Suite E4-545
Boulder, CO 80302

Editing by Melanie Mulhall, Dragonheart
www.DragonheartWritingandEditing.com
Cover Design by Jeff Fuller
www.shelfish.weebly.com
Interior design by Lora Zorian
Graphics by Scott Merriam
www.scottmerriamdesign.com

Printed in the United States of America

First Edition

CONTENTS

FOREWORD

To truly understand the value of strategic agility and the concepts you'll read about in this book, imagine what's involved in executing a four-way, coast-to-coast merger, across thirteen separate locations employing about a thousand people. Further, imagine that the merging businesses are all very entrepreneurial and have widely disparate systems, cultures, and approaches to leadership and management. Each business has between seventy-five and three hundred people, with annual gross revenues ranging from $15 million to $50 million. These are cutting edge veterinary hospitals providing board certified care and emergency services to pets and their human companions around the clock, twenty-four hours a day and every day of the year. Finally, imagine that the organization's strategy is being led by a veterinarian with a good deal of business experience but whose lack of formal training in strategy leads him to refer to himself as an "accidental strategist."

Well, I'm the accidental strategist, and the challenges noted above are exactly the ones I was facing when I first met Dan Montgomery. The strategy team's entire headcount was one—me. I needed strategy that was at least nimble, if not agile. I was searching for some fundamental strategy insights and tools. Attending a national conference for strategists was one of my first orders of business. I might not have known much about strategy, but I realized that, and I also knew that I needed to know more about what I didn't know. Sitting in presentation after presentation, I could see that many of the tools and frameworks being described were quite complicated or perhaps only available to organizations with vast resources at their disposal (think Fortune 500, or large governmental or nongovernmental organizations).

Within just a few minutes, I knew Dan's approach was refreshingly different and that Dan was the sort of strategy advisor we needed. One example that truly resonated with me was an exercise Dan led having to do with capacity overload, a very real and human challenge faced by many of our organizations and many of us as individuals. This exercise drove home the concept that our teams need different approaches to work if we're going to succeed, and simply piling on more work or increasing the pace won't produce sustainable gains for our organizations.

After the presentation, I went up to chat with Dan and realized my good fortune in that we were both living and working in the Front Range of Colorado. I immediately resolved to enlist Dan as a strategy consultant for our new company, hoping that his consulting approach would be as well-grounded as the concepts he had presented. I wasn't disappointed. Through a variety of consulting projects with Dan, our strategy journey became much more concrete, and we've also enjoyed a friendship focused on how to develop and apply real-world strategy.

Dan talks about starting less and finishing more. That resonated with our managers so much that I like to say it went viral in the organization. In meetings all around the company, managers were repeating "Start less, finish more" and asking great questions about how we could accomplish this. Dan's message to start less and finish more often triggers conversations about the negative and positive impacts strategy can have on humans—negative when people are suffering from the very real and dispiriting impacts of initiative overload and positive when we all realize and experience the sense of meaning achieved through the actual completion of work.

Simply put, our people were hungry for tools and concepts about how to get work done in today's increasingly complex, complicated, and chaotic world. I'm guessing that people in your organization have the same hunger.

And as I found at the strategy conference several years back, tools and concepts don't matter if they're out of your organization's reach or even just not accessible to your frontline people and teams. Paraphrasing Ram Charan, I like to say that strategy is everyone's business. And strategy shouldn't be an academic exercise. Instead, it needs to work in spite of the messiness and limitations of the real world. Even better is strategy that works well with and takes advantage of those real-world challenges. Dan's approach makes the concepts and tools of strategy completely accessible to everyone, from executives to team members working on the front lines. This ability to make strategy accessible and useful is quite uncommon in my experience.

The tools you're going to read about are valuable, but Dan's insights are invaluable, which is to say that they are the stuff of true strategy. I think you'll agree once you've finished *Start Less, Finish More*, even if your strategy journey is as accidental as mine.

BRIAN CASSELL, DVM
Chief Strategy Officer
Ethos Veterinary Health

INTRODUCTION

In twenty years of management consulting, I've worked with technology firms, banks, government agencies, utilities, and nonprofits, with clients ranging from the Sisters of St. Martha to the United States Marine Corps. While there are some big differences among industries, I see more similarities. Strategic thinking is difficult for all of us. It requires you to step back from the day-to-day speed and distraction of your job, look around, and ponder deeper questions.

- How is your environment changing?
- What do you value?
- What's your vision of the future?
- Who are your customers and stakeholders?
- How do you provide value for them?

Real strategic thinking challenges a natural human tendency, rooted in the very way our brains work, to stick to the tried and true. These well-worn grooves, or ruts, shape what we see and what we think is possible. We assume we know who our customers are and what they want. We figure that what worked yesterday will work tomorrow. No matter what kind of organization you lead or work in, this is no longer good enough.

For businesses, the competitive playing field is constantly shifting. And for government agencies and nonprofits, there is a need to demonstrate how you provide value in an atmosphere of changing needs and expectations. Rising to these challenges requires *strategic agility*—the capacity to sense change, disruption, and opportunity and respond quickly and forcefully.

At the same time, the evolution of life and business in the past 150 years has created an unprecedented level of complexity in organizations, with a tangle of formalized systems, rules, and processes. This level of bureaucracy, however well intended, makes it ever more difficult to change direction. It dooms organizations that can't change fast enough. It creates a sense of overwhelm, of trying to do too much at a time, and of not knowing where to start.

Legend tells us that Alexander the Great conquered the ancient kingdom of Phrygia by winning a challenge to undo the Gordian Knot, a tangle of incomprehensible complexity. Rather than try to figure out how to untie it, he just drew his sword and sliced it in half. And it came undone. While you might need to employ a more nuanced approach at the office, the principle is the same. You can't untangle complexity by figuring out every thread. You need a way to start simply and boldly and move forward one step at a time.

The essence of the agile mindset and of strategic agility is the principle I call *start less, finish more*. The combination of uncertainty, complexity, and general overwhelm that we all face makes it unproductive, if not impossible, to fully figure out the right course of action in advance. This is a big problem when it comes to strategic planning, which has us trying to project our business three to five years into a hazy future. Strategic agility means having a clear vision of where you're leading your organization while remaining open and flexible about how you get there. You spend less time up front designing the plan and more time iterating and adapting as you go along. You start by actually doing less planning, and in the end, you've built the capacity to adapt quickly and collaboratively as an organization.

This book presents a lot of tools you can use, but the biggest thing I want you to remember is not a tool, it's an insight (and you will find it in the first chapter). Here it is: We limit our ability to think strategically because we dread uncertainty. We retreat into cozy mental models—the habitual ways we observe the world around us—that keep us from seeing a bigger picture of what is possible. The second chapter is about what strategy is, particularly the important distinction between strategic thinking and strategic planning, which are two very different things. From there, we'll explore the five-step Agile Strategy Management process. This includes tools for bringing strategic thinking into a regular cycle of planning, goal setting, action, and learning.

One of the biggest and most unfortunate misunderstandings about business strategy is that it's a subject that can only be understood by experts in shiny shoes and dark suits. I used to think so myself. When I was in business school, strategy was my least favorite subject. It struck me as something bloodless, abstract, and analytical, focused coldly on money. It didn't offer anything I could use in my everyday work to get things done. It took me a few years to see that strategy is really much more interesting than that. It's holistic—a big view of your organization that includes your offer to customers, the external environment in which that offer provides value, and the alignment of systems, processes, financial resources, and people to deliver it. There's the logic of how you position your company in the market and develop products that deliver value, but there's also the more emotional side. That's about creating an organization that inspires and motivates the people who come to work there every day.

Most of us engage in strategic thinking every day. Everyday strategy is a matter of assessing the landscape, focusing on what you want to happen, committing to specific steps, acting, and learning from your experience. People have been doing this forever. Here's an example.

After attempting golf with little discipline or commitment when I was young, I finally took up the game in earnest about twenty years ago, and I found it very challenging. I was out playing with a business associate one day fifteen years ago. After watching me slice two tee shots to an almost identical spot out in the deep rough, he offered me an observation. "Dan, it's as if I can see you change your mind near the top of your backswing. You've got to just commit to the shot and do it!"

That's been one of the hardest lessons for me. I tend to think too much, question my last decision, and physically choke up when it's time to just do it.

The practice of golf requires the ability to learn from the last shot, let go of critical self-talk, and step up to the next one with a clear mind and heart. That's why I like watching the pros. Every shot goes through the following sequence:

1. ASSESS: Survey the landscape. Read the wind and the condition of the course.
2. FOCUS: Choose your strategy for the hole. Where do you want the ball to land on the next shot? What would the shot after that look like? Pick your club.
3. COMMIT: Make your practice swing and take your stance. Let go of any thought about how you might make the shot differently. Relax and feel your feet on the ground. Take a deep breath.

4. **ACT**: Staying focused on the basics—head down, weight shift, wrist action—get moving and execute the shot. The pros call this *pulling the trigger*. Don't start looking up to see where the ball is going before you hit it. For well-practiced golfers, this is baked into muscle memory.

5. **LEARN**: Observe what happened. If you're not satisfied with the results, consider what you would have done differently. Often, you'll see a pro take a practice swing *after* they've hit the ball just to drill that into their muscle memory.

Figure 1: Five Steps to Agile Strategy

Although I describe this as a sequence of five steps, they all blend together in one relatively fast sequence, a single stroke that is one of many in a bigger game.

We use the enso as background for the illustration of this cycle. In Japanese Zen practice, the enso is a circle that is hand drawn in one uninhibited brushstroke to express a moment when the mind is free to let the body act spontaneously and confidently. The circle is open, allowing for movement and development. The enso is a powerful symbol for empowerment and creativity.

HOW I CAME TO WRITE THIS BOOK

All my life I've been fascinated with how organizations tick. Human resources seemed like a natural place to start my career. Along the way, I became fascinated with how computers could be used to create a model of an organization. This led me into a fifteen-year management career in information technology. Later, I got interested in the bigger questions of strategy and leadership and discovered the power of balanced scorecard as a strategy management tool. Strategy management is a body of knowledge and practice that combines the formulation of strategy with execution. The most brilliant strategy is useless if it can't be implemented, and strategy execution must address issues of leadership, organization development, and project management. Balanced scorecard was the first comprehensive approach to strategy management because it was based on developing a shared understanding of how people, systems, and business processes all worked together to create value for a customer and financial results for owners.

During this period, I also had the good fortune to fall in with a group of friends who organized conferences with some of the leading lights in the world of organizational learning. This field is the basis of contemporary leadership development and coaching. Organizational learning draws insights from neuroscience and addresses how we view our world, frame our choices, have effective dialogue, and build high-performing teams.

Something new and unsettling piqued my interest four years ago. At that point, I had developed strategic plans for dozens of clients over a period of fifteen years. As I engaged in follow-up conversations with my clients, a disturbing pattern emerged. The process I had been leading, along with everyone else I knew in the strategy consulting business, spent too much time on a lengthy up-front design process and not enough time on the real work of implementation. We were engaging the workforce in the design process, which was good, and we were leaving our clients with an extremely thorough plan. More often than not, though, the momentum required to keep the plan relevant and moving forward wasn't there. When I asked, many of my clients told me they had employed various hacks to simplify the process. Most of these involved focusing on only a critical handful of measures and taking on fewer initiatives at a time.

At the same time, I was exposed to the emerging world of agile software development. *Agile*, capitalized, is the term used for project and workflow management practices that have revolutionized how software is built over the past twenty years. Agile has been greatly influenced by organizational learning practices. Although Agile is focused on operational execution, it struck me that many Agile insights and practices can be applied to strategic planning and execution. It addressed a lot of problems I'd seen in my IT career with projects involving a lot of up-front design that delivered little value in the end.

WHY AGILE WAS A BIG STEP FORWARD FOR IT

During my IT career, I spent several years working on a project that ultimately went nowhere. I was on a team that was designing a new social services system from scratch in a poor state. In fact, the state was facing an economic meltdown. It was believed that the welfare system would soon be overwhelmed by people who had exhausted their unemployment benefits and would have nowhere else to go. It was the early 1990s, and large organizations were moving away from mainframe computers to the new client-server architecture that made use of personal computers. No one on the team actually had any experience with client-server architecture, but the business case for the new system assumed that it could be delivered much more cheaply with client-server architecture than with a mainframe solution. It was estimated that the entire project would cost four million dollars to build and roll out to forty offices spread over a large geographic area. This assessment proved to be very wrong.

The immediate need was simply to quickly provide income assistance to families who needed it. But the scope soon grew to support every function in the department. Before a line of code was written, we spent eighteen months analyzing and redesigning every function of the entire department, including adoptions and child welfare.

The project was behind schedule from the beginning. Every couple of months, we revised detailed project plans that went three years into the future, predicting what we would be doing many months in advance. After several of these revisions, the original project leader who had created the four-million-dollar business case was replaced. The large systems integrator I worked for assumed the management role in the project. Soon there was a team of over ninety people, mostly external consultants who flew in every Monday morning and out every Friday afternoon. After another year and a half, it was decided that it was time to revisit the original business case. I was tasked with pricing the rollout of the new system, including the deployment of equipment, training, and user support.

By the time I was done, I estimated that the cost of the rollout alone was six million dollars, 50 percent more than the original estimate for the *entire* project. This did not include the revised costs for programming, testing, maintenance, and operations. The new projection for the total cost swelled to twenty-two million dollars. Shortly after this revised estimate, three years after the original business case, the government shelved the project. They couldn't afford it. Millions of dollars sunk into the project had to be written off. Not a single family got food or a roof over their head as a result. Social workers were coping with the bulging welfare rolls without the benefit of the new system.

If we had known about Agile, we would have done a lot of things differently. We would have focused on one small set of features at a time, built a prototype, tested it, and tried it out with a few caseworkers before moving on to the next set of features. We would have ensured that each slice of functionality—for example, reducing the time it took to get food for a hungry family—was creating positive outcomes before moving on. We would have attacked the most important priorities first and delivered on them, so that even if the project was curtailed later, there would be some benefit to real people.

We could have started less and finished a lot more.

Agile practitioners had learned how to start less and finish more in some very specific and practical ways. Dealing with the mind-numbing complexity of big software projects on a daily basis, they had rejected writing detailed plans in favor of a more adaptive approach. I put my old ways aside and embarked on a deep dive into the world of Agile. I wanted to find out how many of the practices in the Agile toolbox could be applied to the work of strategy management. I was able to leverage my years of IT experience and work as an Agile coach for a time. What I discovered is that while Agile techniques build what we might call *operational agility*—the ability to continuously deliver new products and services in response to changing customer needs—the Agile playbook does not address *strategic agility*. Every Agile model I'd seen assumed that strategic priorities came from somewhere outside the diagram. The Agile model was necessary but not sufficient. My quest could not end until I addressed strategic agility.

By discovering objectives and key results (OKRs), I found the link between strategy and operational execution. Here was a work management practice that had a deep kinship with Agile but had a simpler format that was applicable to all business functions at every level in the organization. It was a simple, fast-cadenced goal-setting process that built agility, employee engagement, and learning. Most importantly, OKRs built alignment with strategy throughout the organization. It was an approach baked into Google's growth strategy from the beginning and has since been adopted by other Silicon Valley firms, including LinkedIn, Intuit, and Adobe.

Today, OKRs are being embraced in other kinds of companies like Walmart, Target, *The Guardian*, Dun and Bradstreet, and ING Bank, and increasingly by nonprofits and government agencies. My OKR clients are predominantly in service sectors like health care, hospitality, and municipal government.

THIS BOOK IS A TOOLKIT

On average, there are two English-language business strategy books published every day. Against this humbling background, my intention has been to create a book that feels accessible and useful to owners, leaders, and strategy specialists in small and mid-sized businesses, nonprofits, and government agencies. I have no desire to make this an academic tome. I want this to be a book you would pick up and put in your briefcase for an airplane trip. I want people to read it, challenge their mindset and expectations about strategic planning, and think about which practices they can apply in their organizations.

I've read an enormous amount of business literature in the past twenty-five years or so while I've developed the point of view and practices in this book. You'll find a few of the more important books in the bibliography. The challenge with a lot of that literature is that it's written by academics, drawing on research from big public companies. Instead, I like to focus on the experience of leaders, not abstract research. I want to demystify strategy. The stories in this book are not based on data-crunching research or interviews with Fortune 500 executives who have a public relations agenda. They are drawn from people and organizations I've met and worked with, people who might be just like you.

I'm also a bit of a history geek, so there are a few historical anecdotes here. Since strategy is always based on a hypothesis about the future, it is very instructive to look to the past and see how people thought about the future back then. Since we have the benefit of knowing how things turned out, it's easy to learn from the fallacies in our ancestors' thinking. The biggest problem we have is assuming that the future will look like the present, only more so. Some of the time, that is true. Some of the time, it's not.

The stories in this book illustrate that there is no single prescription for how to build strategic agility. Think of this as a toolkit. The tool you choose depends on the job you have to do. Strategic agility is holistic. It starts with a radical focus on what your customers value. It builds on shared strategic awareness throughout the organization. It requires an orientation towards measurable business outcomes. It must be based on a culture of open, healthy dialogue. And finally, recognizing that none of us can predict the future, it is built on a foundation of fast cycles of experimentation, feedback, and learning—the practice of objectives and key results.

1 | EMBRACING UNCERTAINTY

I N THE LATE NINETEENTH CENTURY, large cities everywhere were dependent on horses for transportation. In New York City in 1894, there were over 100,000 working horses producing an estimated two-and-a-half million pounds of manure per day. At an urban planning conference held in New York that year, it was projected that by 1920, Manhattan would be twenty feet deep in horse droppings. Obviously, this never came to pass, not because New York developed a better strategy for horse manure removal, but because of the arrival and rapid adoption of motor cars—a development that was never considered in the assessment. Horse manure problem solved!

The urban planners suffered from what Chris Argyris called skilled incompetence. They knew so much about the horse-powered urban economy that they lacked the capacity to be open to new possibilities that eventually changed everything. As Suzuki Roshi put it, "In the beginner's mind there are many possibilities. In the expert's there are few."[1]

Industry-shaking disruptions often begin just outside the boundaries we pay attention to, with weak signals that escape detection or seem irrelevant. At the time of that urban planning conference, for instance, Henry Ford was a thirty-year-old engineer working for Detroit Edison and tinkering with his first gasoline-powered buggy in his garage. He would not attract much attention or any investment until 1899. He went bankrupt, reincorporated, and introduced the Model T in 1908. Back in 1894, you might have easily dismissed the automobile as an irrelevant curiosity—if you had even heard of it.

We have a mistaken belief that we can eliminate uncertainty by coming up with a detailed forecast of the future. Extrapolating a current trend and putting a stake in the ground as to what will be trending in five years is a classic case of false precision. This is why so many venture capitalists have rejected the standard business plans that entrepreneurs once used. These plans forecasted the future sales of a product that hadn't even been fully designed, much less built.

Today's trends are not future reality.

Forecasting is a worthy exercise, but it must be undertaken with awareness of its limitations. Today's trends are not future reality, they are assertions about the present. Linear extrapolation of current trends can lead to ludicrous conclusions, like projecting the depth of horse manure in the streets twenty-five years into the future. If you simply project future activity based on current trends, you may miss the weak signals. These are the subtle, emerging bits of information that don't fit your current model about the world but may sneak up behind and surprise you. This bias toward missing the weak signals is compounded further if you only make an assessment every few years. In that case, your view of reality is guaranteed to be wrong, and more wrong as time goes by. Embracing uncertainty means being open to multiple possible futures rather than fixating on one possibility and taking it as a reliable prediction.

THE TRAP OF MENTAL MODELS

Deeply ingrained habits of thinking keep us from seeing emerging insights, opportunities, and risks. Beginning in school and on into the workplace, those who get rewarded with good grades and promotions are the ones who confidently know the answers, or at least appear to. Asking questions, especially difficult ones, is less appreciated. In business, leaders are expected to have a clear view of the horizon and plan accordingly. But our views of what is, and what is possible, are conditioned by assumptions that are often semiconscious or even unknown to us. These assumptions may or may not be true. Our assumptions about the world not only influence how and what we see, they also inform our choices. These assumptions are mental models, verbal and visual patterns generated in our brains. Mental models are not reality. But if we are reasonably sane and intelligent, these models may approximate reality enough to allow us to function in the world—assuming that we are open to changing our minds when appropriate.

Our maps have big consequences for our behavior. For example, an Italian cartographer named Paolo Forlani created a map of the world in 1565 that was based on older maps and stories he had heard. While the map of Europe is quite well defined, his treatment of North America is wildly inaccurate. Though a few coastal features are fairly close to where they should be, it's clear that no one who contributed to the map had sailed north of what is now Southern California. On the Forlani map, the California coast curves north and westward, becoming the east coast of China! The interior is largely blank and labeled "Terra Incognita," although one area labeled "Le Sete Cita" referred to the fabled Seven Cities of Gold. Today, that area includes the cities of Albuquerque, Phoenix, and Las Vegas.

This is the map that John Smith had in his possession when he founded Jamestown. How did this map impact his strategy? Was his plan to set down roots in what was then a malarial swamp? Maybe not. Maybe his intention was to establish a base from which to travel by land to China and establish a new trade route while finding gold on the way.

As the saying goes, the map is not the territory.

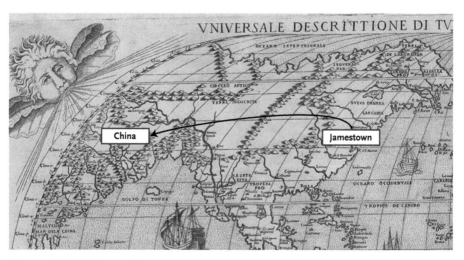

Figure 2: Forlani Map – 1565

Before you can begin setting goals and planning, you need to examine and challenge your map—the assumptions that underlie your business model. This is a key skill in real, in-depth strategic thinking. Too much fixation on one view of the future will blind you to the emergence of new information, opportunities, and risks.

A strategic plan that attempts to predict exactly how everything will unfold is not really a strategy, it's a detailed operational plan or a budget, and it is useful only within a very limited time horizon. Strategic agility, on the other hand, is based on an emotionally inspiring vision of what success will look like, combined with flexible implementation that responds to emerging circumstances.

AGILE DECISION MAKING

In a complex environment, people are continuously doing things they've never done before. How long something will take, what obstacles will be encountered, and what the outcome will be are only known precisely once the work is completed.

In a news briefing in 2002, US Secretary of Defense Donald Rumsfeld commented about the inability to find weapons of mass destruction after invading Iraq.

Reports that say something hasn't happened are always interesting to me because as we know, there are known knowns: there are things we know we know. We also know there are known unknowns: that is to say we know there are some things [we know] we do not know. But there are also unknown unknowns—the ones we don't know we don't know. And if one looks throughout the history of our country and other free countries, it is the latter category that tend to be the difficult ones.[2]

Rumsfeld was widely derided for saying this, given the context. American leadership had pressed for war, confident that Iraq had stockpiles of weapons of mass destruction, but none were found. But the statement is true, per se. In strategic planning, it's critical to acknowledge that we don't know all we wish we did and that there are things we don't even know we don't know that could emerge, like the motor car in the 1890s.

Agile thinkers embrace uncertainty. Embracing uncertainty doesn't mean you just give up and let the wind take you wherever it will. It means that you take a different approach to decision making. The start less, finish more mindset radically reduces the amount of up-front analysis required before a strategy can be undertaken while providing much greater adaptability to change.

Agile thinkers embrace uncertainty.

- Gather just enough information to make necessary decisions. Don't fall into analysis paralysis. It's better to be roughly right, get on with it, and learn from experience. Try the simplest solution first, observe what happens, and then decide on the next step.
- Don't force unknowable details to be elaborated up front. Trying to force the known and the unknown into the same box leads to false precision. This is worse than admitting you don't know.
- Create options to make better decisions later when more is known. Make it part of your regular management calendar to go back and review your assumptions. The more dynamic your industry, the more frequently you should do that review.
- Don't commit to detailed project plans too far into the future. Start with high-level deliverables, known as *epics* in the Agile world, and go through a frequent process of creating detailed work plans for the next iteration only.
- Whenever possible, defer decisions until the last responsible moment. Kicking the can down the road may be the wisest course of action. The last responsible moment is the just-in-time point after which you are causing wasted time for others, bottlenecks, confusion, or risk.
- Centralize control for decisions that are infrequent, that

impact the entire organization, or that have significant economies of scale. This includes enduring parts of the strategy, like organizational purpose and values. It also includes systems and processes that address common functions and efficiencies across the organization, like an accounting system.

- Decentralize all other decisions. If managers and employees throughout the organization understand the purpose, values, and strategy, trust them to do the right thing.

HOW TO THINK ABOUT STRATEGY IN A COMPLEX WORLD

The approach you should take to creating and implementing strategy depends on how much you know about the environment you're operating in, how much you know you don't know, and how likely it is that you don't know what you don't know. This last likelihood—the unknown unknowns—is the essence of a complex environment.

Most professional businesspeople, analysts, and engineers have not been trained or educated to manage strategy in a complex world. Most of us have been trained to operate in what I call a multicausal system. A multicausal system is complicated enough, but given enough data and enough smart people to analyze a defined problem, you can find a workable answer. Because the problem is defined, you know what you don't know. According to Ryan Martens, an Agile pioneer who co-founded Rally Software, on average, civil engineering students solve 3500 problems by the time they graduate. These are all problems that have been predefined and have a correct solution. What engineering students don't learn to do in school is ask the questions that frame the problem in the first place.[3]

Multicausal

Complex

Logic

Cause and effect can be known given enough data and analysis

Cause and effect can only be perceived in retrospect

Action

1. Analyze
2. Predict
3. Plan

1. Probe
2. Sense
3. Respond

Strategy

- Top-down
- 3-5-year cycle
- Plan and predict
- Tightly coupled

- Bottom-up
- Quarterly cycle
- Emergent
- Loosely coupled

Figure 3: Multicausal versus Complex Strategy

A jetliner is a multicausal system. It is optimized for performance under a specific set of conditions that might include a range of temperatures and wind conditions. Although one person may not understand every part of the plane, a group of engineers can. To act strategically in a multicausal system, you proceed by gathering data, analyzing it, and developing a plan of action that you believe will have a high likelihood of success. The goal of such a system is prediction and control of the environment.

This is the world of traditional strategic planning. We call this the *Predict-and-Plan Strategy*. This approach grew out of the automotive industry at a time when there was limited and well-understood competition, when consumer demand could be predicted quite accurately, and when marketing and distribution followed well-established channels.

In a complex system, there are so many variables and network effects that prediction and control become impossible. In this domain, the problem itself is not clear. Engineers often refer to this as a wicked problem. In terms of strategy, this means we don't know what is of most value for our customers, and chances are they don't either. For instance, did you know you needed a smart phone in 2006? I didn't! If we think of strategy as a game plan, the problem is that the rules of the game keep changing unpredictably. Managing strategy under conditions of complexity requires paying constant attention to the market, watching out for competition from unexpected places, continuously imagining possible solutions, making calculated bets, conducting experiments, and observing results. In short, it requires lots more strategic thinking. The focus of strategy shifts from analysis to action and learning.

In a complex world, prediction and control become impossible.

Strategic planning and management are critical in either multi-causal or complex environments but take different forms. Multicausal strategy presumes that we can determine the right way forward ahead of time. And in some cases, perhaps fewer than you might think, the environment is actually predictable enough that we can decide what needs to be done and execute on it.

Complex strategy, on the other hand, requires that we continuously challenge our own mental models and respond to change in real time. Rather than executing a preplanned strategy, we continuously update and validate our strategy by launching short-term experiments. These experiments use OKRs to help us learn what we can produce that customers will value. We call this the *Agile Strategy*.

Agile strategy does not reject the predict-and-plan approach. It includes it in a bigger toolkit that can address both multicausal and complex challenges. The key is to pick the simplest possible approach for each strategic decision. In some situations, it's clear what needs to be done, and the task is to execute efficiently. That's perfect for a predict-and-plan approach. In others, you need a step-by-step process of action and learning. Which approach is best will depend on what industry you're in and where you stand in that industry. Do you need to make bold moves, or is it more important to defend your existing position? You may also apply different levels of agility depending on what part of the organization is involved. Marketing typically calls for more agility than accounting, for example.

The bottom line is that your organization must build the capacity to sense the environment and adapt creatively as needed. This is not a mechanical process. Strategic agility is holistic. It requires both an agile mindset and culture and a disciplined process of strategic thinking, planning, goal setting, and learning.

STRATEGIC PLANNING VERSUS STRATEGIC THINKING

Strategic thinking is something that happens in people's hearts and minds, and it lives and thrives in conversations. Strategic planning is a crystallization of that thinking into a structured process and a document that is inevitably obsolete as soon as it is printed.

Henry Mintzberg of McGill University is one of the wisest and wittiest observers of the world of business strategy. He describes the difference this way: "Formal planning, and the associated forces that encourage it, may discourage the very mental state required to conceive new strategies—a state of openness and easy flexibility that encourages people to step back from operating reality and question accepted beliefs. In short, formal strategic management may prove incompatible with real strategic thinking."[4]

Strategic planning may be hazardous to your health.

Rendering strategy into a plan may, in fact, be hazardous, lulling you into a false sense of security. In my years as a strategy consultant, I've seen three reasons why well-intended strategic planning efforts go bad:

1. The typical detailed three-to-five-year plan can take months to create, but it does not keep up well with change, disruption, and opportunity once completed. This lack of resilience quickly turns a beautifully conceived plan into what we call *shelfware*. Rather than a guide for day-to-day action, these plans are often ignored in the rush of emerging circumstances and the urgency of day-to-day work. They suffer from too much emphasis on up-front design and too little focus on flexible implementation.

2. Strategic planning exercises often do not involve enough of the people who need to carry out the strategy, resulting in

poor understanding and insufficient buy-in. According to the Gallup Organization, only 37 percent of non-management employees "know what their company stands for."[5] Worse yet, a plan created only by senior leaders and consultants may miss important perspectives from the members of the team who are closest to the customers.

3. Detailed long-term plans often generate long lists of projects, creating what we call *initiative overload*—adding more work to an already full plate. Research shows having too many tasks results in none of them being executed well and causes undue stress for team members. Besides, what seems like a good initiative today may not seem like such a good idea a year from now.

Strategy is not a plan to be executed but a hypothesis to be validated.

Strategy is not a plan to be executed but a hypothesis about what your customers value, and it must be continuously validated. Notice the emphasis on customers here. Ultimately, an organization that does not provide value to customers does not survive. This is obvious for private sector businesses, but it also applies to government agencies, although negative impacts may take longer to show up. It certainly applies to nonprofits, which must compete for funding and must demonstrate results.

That's where strategic agility comes in. Agile organizations employ foresight, but they hold their predictions lightly, recognizing that they will inevitably change. They complement foresight with insight, which enables them to more immediately sense and respond to disruption and opportunity. Agile strategy is not something that can be created solely by senior executives and consultants, then executed according to plan. It must engage the collective intelligence and passion of people at all levels in the organization.

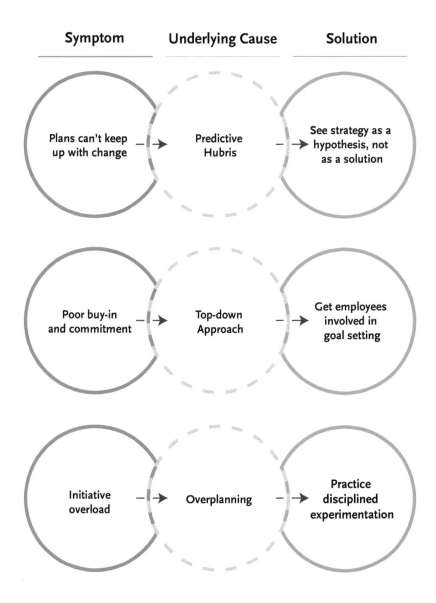

Figure 4: The Trouble with Strategic Planning

From the top of the organization to the bottom, OKRs are the engine that drives strategic agility. OKRs provide a way forward in the face of uncertainty and complexity. In a world where there is no longer such a thing as sustainable competitive advantage, your most important survival skill is the capacity to adapt. This arises from a flexible interplay of strategic thinking and planning. Too often, though, the planning can get in the way of the thinking.

Let's take a closer look at the difference.

2 | STRATEGY

I N THE BOOK OF GENESIS, we are told that the ambitious build-
ers of the Tower of Babel awoke one morning to find that they no
longer spoke the same language. So it is with strategy terminology.
After twenty years in this field, I continue to be astonished by the proliferation of terms describing the basic elements of strategy. In planning sessions, people still find themselves debating the difference
between a mission and a vision. Is a mission really different from
a purpose, or is purpose just a new name for the same old
thing? How are goals different from objectives? Some strategy consultants love to come up with proprietary terms that
make their approach sound new and special. And language
that appeals to the culture of one industry may not resonate
in another.

    There is no one right answer. The important thing is
that you use the terms clearly and consistently in your organization.

*Use
strategy
terms
clearly and
consistently
in your
organization.*

DEFINITIONS

Here are the definitions we'll use in this book:

STRATEGIC THINKING is a personal and interpersonal process of observing emerging signals in your environment, imagining how they might impact your business, and adapting by creating a new vision and strategies.

A STRATEGIC PLAN is a comprehensive document that reflects strategic thinking at a particular point in time. It includes an assessment of the organization's current state, purpose, and values, a vision of the future, strategies for achieving that vision, measurable performance targets, and specific initiatives.

STRATEGY MANAGEMENT is a repeatable business process that links all the elements of a plan into a regular cycle of strategic thinking, action, and learning. This cycle is scheduled in advance but can also be activated when emerging circumstances call for it.

CADENCE is the rhythm of the strategy management cycle, supported by a well-tuned flow of information and conversations. In highly volatile industries, the cadence must be fast; in more stable industries, less so.

STRATEGIC AGILITY is the capacity for your organization to sense change in the environment and adapt in a way that continuously builds value for your customer.

PURPOSE is the reason that the organization exists, the difference that it aims to make in the lives of customers and other stakeholders.

VALUES are standards of behavior and design that guide and constrain the achievement of purpose.

VISION is the desired future state of the organization, three to ten years in the future.

STRATEGIES are three-to-five-year choices about how the organization will sustain itself, grow, innovate, and compete to achieve its vision. There may be multiple, complementary strategies in play at any given time, such as a product strategy, a human resource strategy, and a financial strategy.

MINIMUM VIABLE STRATEGY is a short, elegant expression of the organization's purpose, values, vision, and strategies and the rationale for these. It is persistent, as opposed to the faster iteration of goals, OKRs, and projects.

GOALS are business outcomes targeted for teams or individuals and can last anywhere from one quarter to a year or more. They are measurable and support the strategies.

OBJECTIVES AND KEY RESULTS (OKRS) are a formula for quantifying enterprise-wide vision and strategies or shorter team-level goals. An objective is a qualitative statement of direction, of where you want to go. Key results are quantitative metrics that will tell you if you have arrived.

PROJECTS are individual or collective actions taken to achieve defined business outcomes. They are allocations of people, time, dollars, and other resources. Projects can range from big, capital-intensive initiatives down to daily tasks.

ALTITUDE

Altitude is a concept that helps make a distinction between broad strategic and operational planning and team-level or individual-level goal setting.

These different levels form a spectrum that we call the *strategy stack*. High-altitude strategic elements, like the vision, change infrequently and apply to the entire enterprise. Low-altitude elements, like team-level goals and projects, have a shorter life span. Purpose and values permeate every level, so they are shown along the boundaries of the stack.

Although purpose and values tend to be less measurable, every element inside the strategy stack—the vision, strategies, goals, and projects—can benefit from clearly written OKRs. Visionary OKRs require a three-to-ten-year time span and impact everyone in the organization. Strategic OKRs are the next level down, last a shorter time, such as a year, and potentially involve some people more than others. Goal OKRs are set by teams and individuals for one quarter at a time. Project OKRs are milestones that demonstrate completed work.

Why does altitude matter? Much of the talk about business agility today is about operational agility—addressing lower-altitude issues of work performance and process improvement. The bottom line of operational agility is making and delivering existing products and services in a way that's faster, cheaper, and better. It assumes you already know

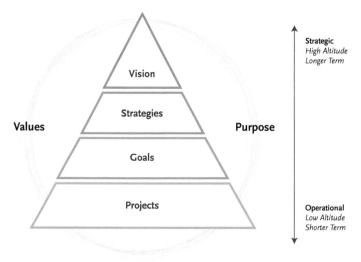

Figure 5: The Strategy Stack

who your customers are and that they can tell you what they need and want. This includes all the practices that go into the software development method known as Agile. Many of these practices have spread to other functions as well, including human resources and marketing. The emphasis in operational agility is on teamwork and flow, team structure, breaking work into small batches accomplished in short sprints, and regular customer feedback. It draws on a culture of open communication, experimentation, and learning. It's a powerful tool.

Strategic agility addresses the larger questions of market innovation and how to develop the game plan when the rules of the game are up for grabs, the field is multidimensional, and you don't always know who your opponents are, let alone have the ability to size them up. It's about adaptability. It requires the kind of strategic thinking that can step back from operations and examine the assumptions that underlie your view of what's possible, given emerging opportunities, or necessary, given looming risks. The sustainability of organizations depends on operational execution in the short run but demands strategic agility in the long run.

Strategic agility addresses the larger questions of market innovation and how to develop the game plan when the rules of the game are up for grabs, the field is multidimensional, and you don't always know who your opponents are, let alone have the ability to size them up.

The human resources department at Sears rolled out OKRs in 2014 and 2015 as a way to improve the productivity of sales associates in its stores. At an operational level, it was a big success, improving performance by a reported 11 percent.

Despite that success, Sears continued to founder, through no fault of its sales associates. Between 2008 and 2018, Sears lost $26 billion in market value, laid off 175,000 people, and closed over 2900 of its 3500 stores. Revenue peaked in 2006 after the acquisition of Kmart, another troubled retailer, and the combined company did not turn a profit after 2010.

What happened? Founded in 1892, Sears, Roebuck and Company was the Amazon of its day, pioneering the use of mail-order purchasing to a largely rural US population. As the nation became more urban, Sears created attractive retail stores in downtown locations, later moving to suburban shopping malls. It created a great stable of brands, including Kenmore appliances, Craftsman tools, and DieHard auto batteries. Sears was a pioneer in the burgeoning credit card industry, introducing the Discover Card in 1985, which was the first to feature cash rewards.

All of these successful innovations are great examples of strategic agility. And the subsequent failures are evidence of a company that lost it. Sears began to fall behind in the 1990s. They failed to adapt to the "big box" retail trend and lost market share to Home Depot and others. They came late to online retailing and lost out to Amazon.

The moral of the story? OKRs are a great execution tool but are of little help if the right vision and strategies are not put in place first.

STRATEGY MANAGEMENT

The vast majority of books written about business strategy are about strategy formulation. This is a big part of the problem: the separation of head and hands. Formulation is the province of senior leaders, consultants, and specialists who arrive at a solution through detailed analysis of data. Having arrived at a brilliant strategy, it is assumed that the troops will all buy in and get on with it. Execution, including communications and project management, is considered a separate project, and it is often neglected. In most organizations, the understanding of strategic priorities decays rapidly the further away you move from the executive suite.

Have you ever heard someone explain a failure by saying that it was a good strategy, just not executed well? It's likely it wasn't a good strategy in the first place. It might have been elegant in its analysis and might have outlined powerful possibilities. But if it didn't consider the leadership required to make it happen, and if that wasn't supported by organizational capacity and culture, business processes and systems, and capital investments, it was a pipe dream.

As Henry Mintzberg put it, when strategy fails, top leadership often blames it on poor implementation by the "dumbbells" lower down on the hierarchy. "Well, those dumbbells down below might well respond: 'If you're so smart, why didn't you take into account the fact that we are dumbbells?' In other words, every failure of implementation is, by definition, a failure of formulation."[6]

Strategy management is a repeatable business process that links formulation and execution into a regular cycle of strategic thinking, action, learning, and adaptation. It emerged as a discipline in the 1990s with the publication of Kaplan and Norton's *The Balanced Scorecard*. The balanced scorecard provided a holistic framework for understanding how investments in people, processes, and technology could be aligned to create customer value and financial performance. This was a brilliant multicausal perspective on strategy execution. But the multicausal mindset behind it has made its utility limited for many organizations, especially complex organizations and fast-moving industries.

Figure 6: Agile Strategy Management Cycle

THE AGILE STRATEGY MANAGEMENT CYCLE

The agile approach to strategy management is designed for complexity. It is a five-step process consisting of assessing, focusing, committing, acting, and learning. And the start less, finish more mindset applies in each stage. The cycle is rapid at the team level and takes longer at the enterprise level, but the steps in the cycle are the same.

Start less, finish more is a core principle at every step of an agile strategy management system. You spend less time in the beginning designing the plan, focusing instead on a minimum viable strategy and iterating from there. In the Commit stage, teams focus on a small number of OKRs at a time to minimize the mental overhead, which is a hallmark of complexity. In the Act stage, minimizing the number of action items on your plate results in more productive work-flow and higher quality.

Strategy management creates a learning cycle of strategy formulation and execution.

1. ASSESSING starts with a collaborative process for observing the landscape, including past performance, as well as opportunities, risks, and disruptions in the environment. This is a place for fresh ideas and perspectives about what is happening. It involves challeng-ing assumptions and mental models about your organization, your competitors, or your customers. Assessing requires very long-term thinking while acknowledging that assumptions about the future may be overthrown in an instant. Rather than trying to exhaustively understand every trend and possibility, you simplify by looking at how these trends impact the people that matter most to you—your customers and other important stakeholders.

2. FOCUSING is an open exploration of possibilities and direc-tions that leads to clear choices about your purpose and your strategic intent. Focusing answers the questions "Why are we here?" and "How will we succeed?" This step results in a simple, elegant statement of direction, the minimum viable strategy. This is a clear vision for the future, supported by purpose and values and carried out through a handful of priority strategies. Focusing looks three to five years into the future. Long-term OKRs are used to make vision and strategies as clear and measurable as possible.

3. COMMITTING is a short-term iterative process for goal setting, creating a fast cycle of disciplined experimentation and learning. Commitments may last from one quarter to one year. Commitments answer questions like "What do we want to achieve in the next quarter? How do we know if we are getting there?" Objectives answer the first question and key results answer the second. Goals, expressed as OKRs, are desired business outcomes set by the teams responsible for achieving them. They provide alignment and communication by linking enterprise-wide objectives and targets with those of the individual team.

4. ACTING is where the rubber meets the road. It answers the questions "Who is doing what? And is it getting done?" Quarterly OKRs are translated into a manageable weekly cadence of projects and tasks to achieve the key results. In today's competitive environment, time is a scarce and highly valuable resource. Big problems or initiatives are broken down into small batches of work that can be completed in a short time, providing feedback and creating value for customers faster.

5. LEARNING completes the cycle. A number of questions are asked and answered in this part of the process: "What did we do right? What would we do differently next time? What have I learned as an individual?" These are the learning questions. Despite our best attempts, we often fail—or sometimes succeed—for unforeseen reasons. This is inevitable when operating under conditions of uncertainty. Validated learning is a rigorous way to use feedback and outcome measures to evaluate progress.

Strategy doesn't have to be a confusing Tower of Babel. Having a common language for talking about strategy invites everyone into the conversation. In agile organizations, strategic thinking, planning, and learning are part of everyone's job description. There is tremendous power in giving the right stakeholders a voice and a vocabulary to create a shared picture of the present and the future.

Let's break down the steps in the cycle and explore each one, beginning with assessing. While we will be looking at each step in a discrete way, in practice, they overlap and flow into each other like a well-planned and executed golf stroke.

3 | ASSESS

S TRATEGIC THINKING IS A PARADOX. It involves long-term thinking, often without a specific end date. And at the same time, it must remain fresh. One of the big problems with strategic planning is that assessment—the generation of insights about the environment—may be conducted only once in the planning cycle, which might be three to five years long. Your customers and competitors don't likely follow this schedule. Your environment might stay relatively stable for a long time but then go through sudden disruptions. In an agile environment, assessment is a fresh and continuous process of sense-making.

ASSUMPTIONS, ASSERTIONS, AND ASSESSMENTS

Our mental models frame our choices, based on what we can imagine is possible. In the world of strategy, mental models about our world are called *planning assumptions*. These assumptions help us make sense of what we see, inspire us, or constrain us. We can't move forward strategically unless we make some assumptions about the reality we are living in. Having said that, the way we usually use the term

There are two kinds of assumptions. Assertions are statements that can be objectively proved. Assessments are matters of subjective opinion and judgment.

_____

assumptions is rather sloppy. There are two distinct categories of assumptions: assertions and assessments. Assertions are statements that can be factually proved or disproved. They can be true or false, but that truth or falsehood is objectively verifiable. For example, the assertion that Earth is flat is false. That we are planted on Earth by gravity is a true assertion. Assertions must be about things in either the past or present to be verifiable. We can't know the future until it arrives—and then, of course, it is no longer the future.

Assessments, on the other hand, are matters of subjective opinion or judgment. They can't be objectively proven to be true or false but can be determined to be grounded or ungrounded through a process of validation. They are often given credence depending on the social status of the person making them. For example, Ken Olsen, the founder of Digital Equipment Corporation and a highly regarded technology innovator, said in 1977, "There is no reason anyone would want a computer in their home."[7] Let's deconstruct this assessment and understand how we might have validated or invalidated it at the time.

The first rule is to be suspicious of any blanket statement that uses terms like *never, always, only, anyone, everyone, no one,* and so forth. Olsen's statement applied to every person on the face of the earth, for all time. The second rule is to be wary of judging a person's motivations by their observable behavior. Olsen assumed that he knew what people would want or not want. But it's a well-established marketing truism that customers often don't know what they want until they see it. Henry Ford apparently understood this because he has been quoted as saying, "If I'd asked my customers what they wanted, they would have said a faster horse."

If you were willing to argue with a well-regarded scientist and business leader, which is what Mr. Olsen was at the time, you might have been able to challenge him with several verifiable assertions. In fact, you could buy a personal computer kit (assembly required) beginning in 1975! So in fact, some people already had computers in their homes in 1977. Admittedly, they weren't very powerful and didn't do anything useful for anyone but a serious computer geek. But you might have noted Intel founder Gordon Moore's 1965 factual observation that the processing power of integrated circuits had doubled every twenty-four months since their invention in 1947. Moore turned this into an assessment, called Moore's Law, that predicted this would continue into the future. So far, it has. It was a well-grounded assessment. Ken Olsen couldn't imagine that any home computer could have the power of one of his DEC minicomputers, but in fact, you now have far more power than that in your phone.

But there's a catch. If Moore's Law continues through 2050, transistors will have to be smaller than a single hydrogen atom, which seems unlikely. Like any mental model, assessments are only relatively true in a particular context for a limited length of time. But we never know how long they will hold true until it becomes clear that they are no longer valid.

Assessments have to do with the future because they influence our view of what's possible and what our choices are. Any prediction about the future is an assessment. Assessments are essential to strategy but must be recognized for what they are.

The problem for strategic leaders comes from confusing assessments with assertions. We take our beliefs to be facts and blindly go forward. Replacing bad assessments with better ones is an ongoing process. For example, I had a client whose CEO had a very common—and ungrounded—assessment that everyone in the organization understood the strategy, which led to the belief that they had talked about it enough and just needed to get it done. Fortunately, a survey revealed that in fact, most of the workforce did not understand the strategy and wanted to know more about it. The "we" who had talked enough about it was the executive team, but understanding of the strategy faded rapidly outside the walls of the executive conference room. The survey led the CEO to revise his assessment and hold a series of town hall meetings to present and discuss the strategy throughout the organization.

Early in my career in IT, there was a common saying that "nobody ever got fired for buying IBM." If it could have been proven true in the past, this would qualify it as an assertion. It became an assessment when it was assumed that this would continue to be true in the future. And why not? Big Blue had been the dominant player in business computing for decades. They were not the most innovative company, but their technology was reliable and well supported by armies of dedicated systems engineers in blue suits.

But the day came when IBM's dominance in big mainframe systems was threatened by Moore's Law, the predicted and very rapid miniaturization of computer chips. This led to a proliferation of microcomputers in business in the 1980s. Most of the world was buying microcomputers with the MS-DOS operating system from Microsoft and making Bill Gates very rich. Trying to catch up from behind, IBM launched a proprietary microcomputer operating system called OS/2.

I worked in a banking data center at the time, and my boss was as loyal an IBM customer as he could be. He had built the IT division from three people to over two hundred as the bank grew, and IBM had provided him with reliable hardware, software, advice, and service every step of the way. They had made his career—until then. Against the advice of my team, which was responsible for microcomputers, he committed to a major rollout of OS/2. We grudgingly went along, but the technology had been rushed to market and not adequately tested. This delayed the rollout of a critical lending application by a year. And my boss was fired.

IDENTIFY MACRO TRENDS USING STEEP

Developing assessments about the future based on current trends is fraught with peril, for reasons we've already talked about. In particular, articles and speeches about technological trends tend to fall into the trap of representing the belief that whatever is going on now has a flavor of inevitability. Technology trends tend to be the most tangible. Often, the advocates of these points of view have financial interests in the outcome. There's no doubt that technological innovation is one of the major drivers of uncertainty and change. But there are others as well:

- SOCIAL: demographic trends, attitudes, behavior, and lifestyles
- TECHNOLOGICAL: tools impacting productivity and driving new business models
- ECONOMIC: international trade, stock market performance, consumer purchasing power, taxes, and interest rates
- ENVIRONMENTAL: climate change, topsoil, water table levels, and pollution
- POLITICAL: legal and regulatory impacts

It is a mistake to create an assessment based on talk about the future. A more useful approach is to go through each social, technological, economic, environmental, and political (STEEP) category and list both what is known with a high degree of certainty and what is unknown. In the case of knowns, for example, it is relatively easy to predict the number of high school graduating seniors in the State of Colorado five years from now. An unknown might be what their political attitudes will be then.

Category	Known	Unknown	Stakeholder Impacts
Social			
Technological			
Economic			
Environmental			
Political			

Table 1: STEEP with Stakeholder Impacts

ASSESS IMPACTS ON CUSTOMERS AND STAKEHOLDERS

There's always a lot going on in the world we could pay attention to, but which trends are most relevant? We need to consider how these likely trends or scenarios will impact the people we most care about—our customers and other stakeholders. The term *stakeholder* is an all-encompassing one, including not only our customers but others whom we impact and who impact us, such as suppliers, regulators, investors, community interest groups, current or potential employees, and even competitors. Any change to the dynamic of the ecosystem or any player in it may require rethinking the strategy. Understanding all the stakeholders is particularly important for nonprofits and government agencies. In the private sector, the customer both pays for and receives the benefit of the product or service. In nonprofits and government entities, donors or taxpayers pay for the service, and the benefits go to a particular target client group.

It might be easy to come up with a long list of stakeholders. But

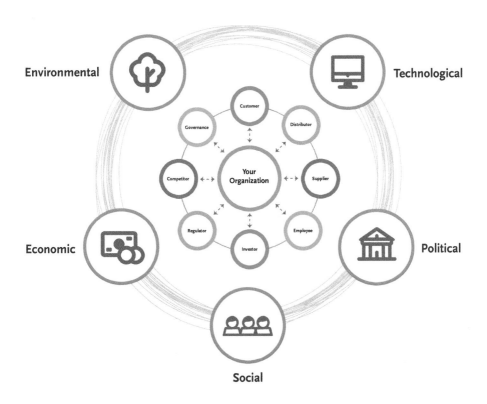

Environmental

Technological

Economic

Political

Social

Customer
Governance
Distributor
Competitor
Your Organization
Supplier
Regulator
Employee
Investor

Figure 7: How Are Your Stakeholders Influenced by Trends?

it is important to make distinctions based on how important each stakeholder is. The most important stakeholders—typically customers, shareholders, and employees—are the ones whose commitment is essential. Then there is a category of stakeholders who are still critical, but less essential, and in some cases, replaceable. These might include regulators, suppliers, bankers—and competitors. Finally, there might be others who are impacted by your decisions. It's good to consider what outcomes this last group of stakeholders would experience from your decisions, whether positive or negative.

Figure 8: Stakeholder Impact

Considering how the macro trends will impact the people who impact you, go back to the STEEP analysis and consider how each trend influences your most critical stakeholders.

It's helpful to create a map of the value you exchange with each stakeholder so you can understand how this might be impacted by external factors as well as your own strategies. Each stakeholder has a two-way relationship with you.

The exchanges of value between the enterprise and its stakeholders may be either tangible or intangible.

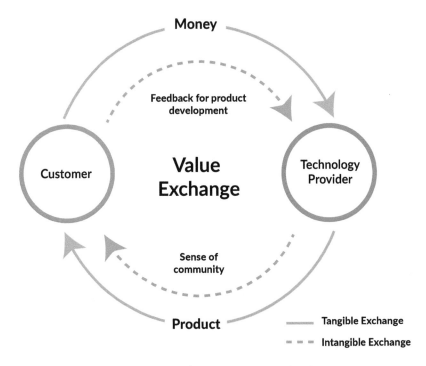

Figure 9: Value Exchange Between Players in a Business Eco-System

- TANGIBLE: specific goods or services exchanged for money, governed by contracts and civil law precedents
- INTANGIBLE: additional value provided in the form of information, emotional factors such as belonging to a community, or other experience

For example, let's say I'm a provider of networking technology. I make products, you give me money, and I give you a product, say, a network router. This is the tangible part of the exchange. The terms of a tangible relationship may be spelled out in a contract. What about the intangible aspects? Let's say you're a network engineer who influences purchasing decisions for this technology. As a technology provider, I create a sense of community for you, as a user, through conferences and social networks that shape your professional identity. You become an expert on this router. Because you have invested a lot in understanding my product and it's a big part of your résumé, you are happy to give me valuable feedback I can use for product development. That is the intangible value of the exchange.

The next step is to put all the exchanges together and rate each in terms of performance. What outcomes do you want from each relationship? What risks are there? What strategies and actions have an impact on the relationship? This can help you target critical areas for improvement that can be translated into strategies and OKRs later.

Stakeholder	What they want, need or value from us	Their assessment of our performance	What we want, need, or value from them	Our assessment of their performance
A				
B				
C				

Table 2: Stakeholder Exchange Assessment

HOW AGILE DO YOU NEED TO BE?

Many business pundits these days like to throw the term *VUCA* around, as in "It's all a VUCA world these days." VUCA stands for volatility, uncertainty, complexity, and ambiguity. It originated in the military to describe the unpredictable dynamics after the end of the

Cold War. In a VUCA world, everything is subject to rapid disruption. The usual message from people who talk about VUCA is apocalyptic: those who don't adapt will surely die without knowing what hit them.

In fact, we are not all in active combat, and VUCA is unevenly distributed. The multicausal, predict-and-plan approach to strategy still works pretty well in some places. This is especially the case in industries with long capital budgeting cycles or heavy regulation and government mandates. These include utilities and pharmaceuticals, as well as government itself. The biggest VUCA victims are industries like technology, media, and retail that are subject to fickle consumers and intense competition. The rest, including health care, are somewhere in between.

The level of VUCA could be described as the temperature of the industry. Higher temperature translates into a higher operational tempo, a term I've borrowed from my military clients. A predict-and-plan strategy might be a good fit with a lower-temperature industry, where vision, strategies, and key performance indicators can and perhaps should remain frozen for many years. Even so, low-temperature environments can benefit from continuous small improvements delivered via OKRs. For instance, in a nuclear power plant, we value efficiency, safety, accuracy, and time, and we will continue to do so for the foreseeable future. Hundreds of people may be dedicated to making sure nothing goes wrong. Even as the high-level strategy remains the same, many of these organizations suffer from the other two big problems of strategic planning: lack of employee buy-in and initiative overload. The quarterly OKR process builds employee engagement with the strategy, builds on the perspective and intelligence of all employees, and involves them in setting goals that inspire them.

Health care is a complex industry with multiple stakeholders and is somewhere in the middle of the VUCA spectrum. The way health care is delivered is changing rapidly, but the basic value of the service stays the same—delivering relief from pain and better treatment outcomes at a reasonable cost. The demand for health care is theoretically infinite, and the supply of new medicines and treatments is increasing rapidly, which has led to spiraling costs. In the US, the patients who receive care typically pay out of pocket for only part of the true cost, with the rest borne by either government or insurance companies. In other countries, health care is paid for out of tax revenues. In either case, demand for health care tends to be greater than supply, leading to upward cost pressures no matter what country you live in.

Michael Kersten, Director, Complex and Serious Illness for the Hill Physicians Medical Group in the San Francisco Bay Area, is applying agile principles to health care. Michael has created a cross-functional team—with skills including pharmacy, nursing, data analysis, palliative care, and various physician specialties—to work with patients who have complex and serious illnesses. The funder of the pilot project, Blue Shield of California, has defined success metrics that include reduced hospital stays and fewer readmissions, so it's clear what outcomes are desirable.

The team is charged with developing new programs to achieve these outcomes. The part of the picture that is truly agile is the way that data is being compiled and reported—a prime example of operational agility supporting a vision of success that's stable over time. The team is continuously finding new ways to view and use the data that provide better support for new programs that improve outcomes. For example, the team looked at different ways to gather and assess data from patients with congestive heart failure. By analyzing rehospitalization rates against predictive indicators that the patients themselves could monitor, they developed a program to make it easy for patients to record and report their own data on weight gain and salt intake.

In defense of the VUCA argument, though, many organizations that believe life is predictable may be in for a surprise. Government agencies are often held up as a case in point. We expect government to change slowly, if at all. But is that actually realistic anymore? Futurist Tom Frey has outlined no less than sixty-three emerging issues that spell turbulence for cities.[8] He predicts that cities will lose over 50 percent of their current revenue streams over the next two decades. Today's sales tax policies and systems are already being buffeted by the triumph of online sales over conventional brick-and-mortar retail. Uberization of personal transportation may lead to drastic declines in auto sales, a major source of tax revenue. Driverless vehicles and drones will have major impacts on urban infrastructure. High levels of income inequality are creating a housing affordability crisis in successful geographies and, at the same time, are preventing people from selling their homes and moving out of less successful areas. Automation is likely to create unprecedented levels of unemployment. Municipal employees will need to be reskilled or lose their jobs.

Even if cities continue to have the same basic mandate twenty years from now, the way they deliver on it will have to change in ways we can't predict. The basic value that a municipal government provides—public safety, economic development, regulation, built infrastructure, and efficient service delivery—may remain the same, but the way it is delivered might be very different. Think about the way that the rapid emergence of automobiles changed cities in the first part of the twentieth century.

SWOT: USE WITH CAUTION

If you are applying the methods offered thus far, you have created a number of planning assumptions that will underlie your strategy:

- A set of relevant trends in the larger environment that might impact your business, including the level of uncertainty or volatility in your industry
- What you know about these trends and what you wish you knew more about
- Who your stakeholders are and how these trends may affect them
- What the key exchanges of value are with each stakeholder and how well you, and they, are performing

Now it's time to summarize it all using the SWOT matrix. SWOT (which stands for strengths, weaknesses, opportunities, and threats) is one of the simplest and most common ways to summarize the key points of a strategic assessment. It's been around since the 1960s. While it can be useful, there's a major flaw to it. People typically go through each of these four categories in order. That is a big mistake. Strengths and weaknesses are relevant only in relation to the organization's larger value-creation strategy and its relationship to external stakeholders. The process should be outside-in, starting with opportunities and threats identified through the STEEP and stakeholder process. After that is done, you can look at the strengths and weaknesses. Thus, a better though unpronounceable term would be OTSW.[9]

I've run dozens of assessment sessions, and from that experience, I've seen that without this external context, strengths become a list of feel-good statements that are not descriptive, like *our employees*, and weaknesses become a poorly disguised wish list featuring phrases like *lack of customer database*. Another flaw is that using bullet points like *our employees* is vague. *What* about our employees is a strength? Will you remember what you said about employees two weeks from now? Using complete sentences is much more specific and useful.

This is especially important because sometimes an assertion or assessment can be both a threat and an opportunity or both a strength and a weakness, depending on how you look at it. For example, *the average tenure of our employees is thirty-five years* is an assertion. You can do the math and prove it. *Our employees are extremely loyal* is a positive assessment, a strength that you might derive from this fact. But wait. They might be staying with your company because they know their skills are out of date and no one else would hire them. Is having an average tenure of thirty-five years a sign that your company is a great place to work at or that you and your employees are stuck in a rut with out-of-date skills? If weaving new skills into your workforce is desirable, you might prefer the average tenure to be considerably less than thirty-five years. The assessments *our employees are extremely loyal* and *our employees' skills are out of date* may both be well-grounded assessments. Don't be afraid of paradoxes. If both of these assessments are valid, the job of strategy is to find a way to accommodate that paradox.

	External	Internal
+	**Opportunities** External trends that we can exploit to our advantage within the bounds of our purpose and governing values	**Strengths** Internal capacities that enable us to mitigate threats and pursue opportunities
−	**Threats** Risks arising from trends outside the organization, including competition and substitute products	**Weaknesses** Internal challenges that detract from our ability to respond to threats or take advantage of opportunities

Table 3: OTSW Summary

What combination of training and strategic hiring could update skills while preserving loyalty?

Threats and opportunities tend to rely more on assessments than assertions because they are about what might happen in the future. What if your assessment is that *Moore's Law will remain true for at least the next five years?* Let's say you are a manufacturer of appliances that use computer chips. What makes it a threat? You might expect competitors to continuously bring appliances with more functionality to the market, requiring you to keep up or potentially lose customers. Or you could view it as an opportunity to potentially get ahead of your competitors by continuously bringing more functionality to the market yourself, faster than your competitors can.

OTSW is useful at every level of the organization. Every unit can benefit from using it to examine the assertions and assessments underlying their contribution to the overall strategy. This is true whether it's a customer-facing team, such as sales, or a support group with internal customers, such as accounting. Every team in the organization needs to develop the muscle for continuous strategic thinking about the trends and stakeholder relationships that matter for them. And the more dynamic your industry—or the environment of a particular team in your organization—the more often the OTSW should be reviewed.

Assessments are difficult to see, especially our own. Assessments are the foundation of our mental models and are often unconscious. Bringing assessments into the light of day and challenging them is hard work. The most effective way to challenge assumptions is on a team that has a high level of trust and open dialogue. Operating in complexity requires tapping in to the intelligence and perspective of everyone on the team, along with as many stakeholders as possible. And when you do that, you have a better chance of starting less and finishing more. Why? Many organizations find assessment not only difficult to do, but time consuming. There are so many possibilities to consider. Agile organizations short-circuit this process by dedicating their attention to how the big trends found in the STEEP analysis may directly impact customers and other critical stakeholders.

4 | FOCUS

F OCUSING IS THE NEXT STAGE of strategic thinking and is
where planning begins. You've developed a routine for sensing
change in the environment. But what will you do about it? Focusing is about making choices. As strategy guru Michael Porter said,
"The essence of strategy is choosing what NOT to do."[10] Focusing
starts with exploring potential ways forward, then making clear decisions about strategic intentions and communicating them to your
team. This includes purpose and values and the higher levels in the
strategy stack, vision and strategies. These are the big goals that apply
to everyone in the organization, the big decisions about where you
will concentrate your resources, and the values that guide individual
and team action. If you're practicing agile strategy management, this
is as far as it goes with three-to-five-year planning. The rest is iterative, taking place in annual or quarterly OKR cycles.

Commander's intent is a military concept that illustrates the idea
of focus. It is a declaration by the leader about what a successful battle
will look like. It describes why the mission is being undertaken and
what a successful conclusion looks like. It provides guidelines that
empower subordinates to adapt to the chaos of battle. The communication of commander's intent was a major reason that the allied

invasion of Europe was successful on D-Day. After years of planning, the reality on the ground on June 6 was different from what had been anticipated in the planning process. The weather was bad. Communications systems broke down. But everyone understood that the major objectives were to form into ad hoc units and seize bridges, road junctions, and other key areas. Soldiers improvised, and the mission was successful.

This is not a new idea. The first known strategy author, Sun Tzu, lived during a chaotic period called the Warring States in fifth century BCE China. He hired himself out as a military strategist and trainer for various warlords, and he wrote a book titled *The Art of War* to document his methods. He saw the world, and the battlefield, as an ever-shifting, complex interplay of forces that were inherently unpredictable. Sun Tzu always had a broad mission in mind. Of course, you go into battle with a plan, but you need to expect the unexpected. Let less critical objectives change and develop spontaneously.

Agile leaders create a clear picture of success in the minds of their followers but are vigilant observers of the unexpected.

Sun Tzu provided examples of how a wise commander could exploit emerging factors to reshape the battlefield to his advantage. The commander might find himself on a high place with loose boulders and set them raining down on the enemy below. He might observe the cycle of a tidal river and build a dam that holds the water back until the moment the enemy is crossing, then destroy it. Timing, according to Sun Tzu, was crucial. On-the-spot insight was every bit as essential as planning and foresight. The biggest enemy the leader could face was what Sun Tzu called fixation, which meant having a set idea of what you think is going on—a mental model—that keeps you from recognizing opportunities and threats in the moment.

But the larger mission was always more important than the battle, according to Sun Tzu. He did not believe that victory was simply about destroying the enemy. "One hundred victories in one hundred battles is not the most skillful," Sun Tzu said. "Subduing the other's military without battle is the most skillful." His emphasis was on achieving victory while keeping as many resources intact as possible. In modern business language, this is creating the most value with the least investment.[11]

Agile leaders create a clear picture of success in the minds of their followers but are vigilant observers of the unexpected.

MINIMUM VIABLE STRATEGY

In the world of Agile software development, a *minimum viable product* is one involving the smallest set of features requiring the least amount of work that will get you the most information about what your customers value. I've borrowed this idea and applied it to strategy. Rather than a detailed plan that inevitably decays as soon as it's written, a *minimum viable strategy* is a statement of intent that addresses only the foundations: purpose, values, vision, and a small handful of strategic priorities. It should fit on one page—or better yet, a poster. Don't get bogged down writing a lengthy document—shelfware—that will be out of date as soon as it's distributed. The best strategy is the most economical in terms of the time it takes to create it, the ease with which it can be updated, and the simplicity of communicating it.

Since we are making the claim that strategy has to be iterative, every level of the strategy is, in fact, an experiment and a choice. A minimum viable strategy must provide the clearest, simplest, and most actionable declaration of why the organization exists, as well as the values, design principles, and high-level priorities that provide guidance for everyone in it. The high-level elements of strategy that we develop in the Focus stage are those that apply to the entire enterprise, are long-term, and tend to be more aspirational and less precisely measurable. These need to be centralized to provide coherence for the whole organization. In an agile organization, everything else should be iterative and decentralized. Local decisions almost always benefit from better local information. And while decentralization introduces some inefficiencies, this matters less than the advantage of faster response time.

PURPOSE

Why does your organization exist? What difference would it make if it didn't? A statement like *we want to make a lot of money* is not a purpose, though it might be a desirable result. Purpose is a long-term proposition, never fully reached, that describes the value your enterprise produces for the world. It is a direction, not an endpoint. Purpose and mission are often used interchangeably, with purpose being the more popular term lately. This is probably because the world has seen a lot of badly worded mission statements that conveyed very little value. The term *mission* also suffers from semantic confusion depending on the setting. For example, in the military, a mission is a short-term activity with a clearly defined endpoint. We'll use the term *purpose* here. The purpose should live deep in the organization's DNA. Google's purpose from the outset has been "To organize the world's information and make it universally accessible and useful." That covers a lot of territory and defines the scope for many lines of business, from search engines to driverless cars. There was some talk in 2014 about changing it, but in fact, this statement has been in place now since 1998. An unambiguous purpose statement should include the following:

- The organization's primary customer or most important stakeholder group
- The outcome or benefit that the organization provides to that customer
- Constraints or boundaries of the organization's scope of operations or ethical standards

Here is the easiest format to follow: Our purpose is to provide (whom) with (outcome or benefit) through (product or service) while (staying within constraints or boundaries).

Alfred P. Sloan's statement of purpose for General Motors, written in the 1920s, said "General Motors exists to make money by making motor cars." The primary constituency, implied but not stated, is shareholders. The outcome for shareholders is profitability. GM will make motor cars. It is not in the railroad business. Similarly, Google's purpose has an implied customer—the users of information. The outcome is to make this information more useful and accessible. And the constraint is that Google is primarily in the business of organizing information. If they start manufacturing cars, the purpose will need to be reworded.

Developing a simple purpose is harder than it looks. There's often a tendency to attempt being all things to all people, but that kind of statement provides no focus for priorities or decision making.

VALUES

Beginning with Plato, philosophers have declared that there are three principal values from which all other values are derived: Beauty, Truth, and Goodness. Beauty is the realm of artistic appreciation, creativity, and design. Truth is objective knowledge, the degree to which our mental models match reality. And Goodness includes ethics, care, and service to others. The ancient Greeks saw these three principles as dynamically interconnected, though modern thinking tends to divorce them from each other. Beauty has become an altar on which goods are often sold, but beauty in the form of art is often viewed as a luxury. Truth is based on materialistic science, with economics—the aptly named dismal science—reducing business to tangible exchanges between supposedly rational actors. The concept of Goodness is often relegated to the realms of theology, philosophy, and ethics. The core values in almost all strategic plans are exclusively ethical principles.[12]

Some exceptional companies have reunited the three Platonic values. In 2013, Apple, known for its commitment to quality design, introduced three values: simplify, perfect, delight. They declared a commitment to beauty—the aesthetic value of their products—and to the goodness of their company's impact on the customer. The quest to perfect demands a commitment to the truth that the product works intuitively and elegantly. Whether intended or not, Apple has committed to the Platonic values of Beauty, Truth, and Goodness.

The best values link ethics with business design values—what to make, how to make it, who to sell it to—and acknowledge the company's intention to act positively towards stakeholders and the environment. In too many cases, though, values are *lobbyware*, ethical pleasantries that look good on a plaque in the lobby. Enron is a classic case of a company that had a fine-sounding set of values but didn't follow them. Their values included communication, respect, integrity, and excellence. What was important was the values they didn't state, such as maximizing quarterly earnings at all cost to boost share price. That was what truly motivated the leadership of the company. You could call it a stealth value, and one that was actually more important than the stated values. Ultimately, this dishonesty destroyed the company.

Whole Foods is a positive example. Their website lists eight core values with a description of what each means, along with the standards they use to measure performance on each of them. For example, the value statement "We sell the highest quality natural and organic products available" is backed up by lists of unacceptable food ingredients. There are specific definitions of what it means for produce to be responsibly grown, as well as standards for animal welfare and sustainable seafood. The company's commitment to measuring how they live their values means that they are addressing both the good and the true. Their eight core values speak directly to the value they provide to all their stakeholders. And unlike Enron, Whole Foods is honest about the bottom line: "We create wealth through profits and growth."[13]

It can be tempting to treat core values as another box to check off on a list of strategic planning to-dos. But values cannot be rattled off in a quick exercise and pasted into the strategic plan. They must be well understood and reinforced consistently by the leadership team. Values provide simple rules for decision making. They create cultural cohesion across the entire organization, where many people are making decisions independently of each other. Simple rules solve what I referred to earlier as the shelfware problem of traditional strategic plans—plans that begin to gather dust as soon as they are created. As strategy authors Donald Sull and Kathleen M. Eisenhardt put it, "Strategies don't live in thick binders—that's where they go to die. Simple rules, in contrast, represent the beating heart of strategy."[14] Complex situations create many possible courses of action, which can confound employees on the front line. Values expressed as simple rules make it easier for everyone to act confidently.

The four values of the Agile Manifesto, developed by a group of innovative software programmers in 2001, embody this idea.

MANIFESTO FOR AGILE SOFTWARE DEVELOPMENT

We are uncovering better ways of developing software by doing it and helping others do it. Through this work we have come to value:

INDIVIDUALS AND INTERACTIONS over processes and tools
WORKING SOFTWARE over comprehensive documentation
CUSTOMER COLLABORATION over contract negotiation
RESPONDING TO CHANGE over following a plan

That is, while there is value in the items on the right, we value the items on the left more.

The authors of the Manifesto started off with a statement of purpose: developing better ways to build software that others could use as well. So the primary customers are software developers, and the benefit is a better way to write software. The primary constraint is that it's about software. It's not about marketing or recruiting employees, even though these values have since been modified and applied to functions outside of IT. The four values provide a framework for making decisions. Relationships with people are more important than following a defined process. It's better to build something that works than to spend time writing technical manuals. Open, trusting relationships with customers are more important than sticking to the letter of a contract. And any plan must be adapted to emerging circumstances.[15]

Whatever your company's values are, it is important to articulate them in writing. Don't just list them, describe how they should guide behavior. Real life is ambiguous, and it's often hard to know the right thing to do. Real values—those that are authentically at the company's foundation and not just lobbyware—will help everyone, at every level in the organization, understand how to behave in a way that's consistent across distance and time. This reduces the stress that complexity causes. Instead of feeling distracted by confusion, you make the choice that best fits with your overall values. This simplicity of attention is the essence of start less, finish more.

VISION

Vision is a description of a particular point in the future, an immediate compass heading on the long-term journey defined by the purpose. It describes what success looks like three to ten years in the future. It should be brief, easy to understand and communicate, measurable, and emotionally inspiring. Perhaps the greatest modern prototype vision statement is still John F. Kennedy's declaration made to a joint session of Congress on May 25, 1961: "This nation should commit itself to achieving the goal, before this decade is out, of landing a man on the Moon and returning him safely to the Earth." It was inspiring and the mother of all stretch goals. No one knew exactly how to achieve it at the time. At the same time, it was not slippery. It was specific, measurable, time-bound, and a bold commitment because success or failure would be obvious. People had imagined it for centuries, but no one, including Kennedy, actually knew how to do it. And it was achieved on July 20, 1969.

I've seen a lot of vision statements that were either a repackaging of the mission statement or a cute slogan, what I call a bumper

WATCH OUT FOR WEASEL WORDS!

Weasel words are used to create vague, ambiguous statements that lack real meaning. All too common in both politics and strategic planning, they are a convenient way to avoid any meaningful choice or commitment. The words sound impressive but are actually slippery, superficial, and lacking in substance. This jargon does not inspire and provides no recognizable definition of success. Here's an example of a vision statement from an unnamed logistics and distribution company. Can you pick out the weasel words?

Utilizing the peak performance of our greatest resource—Our People!—we will leverage world-class information technology solutions to achieve innovative customer-centric supply chain synergies.

Peak performance is the quintessence of jargon. Who doesn't want peak performance? Will unrelenting peak performance lead to burnout? Better to define desired results more specifically.

Calling out **Our People!** with capital letters and an exclamation point and calling them our greatest resource is a pathetic attempt to show how much we care without any specific commitment to improving the workplace.

While **leverage** is an actual verb, it is meaningless in this context. Leverage to what end?

Same with **world class**. How do we know if our IT solutions are world class, and how does that actually benefit our customers?

Who doesn't want to be **innovative**?

What exactly are **customer-centric supply chain synergies**, and how do we know if we have them?

And by when exactly will all this occur?

This statement fails to put any stake in the ground against which future performance can be measured, and it's far too confusing to inspire anyone!

sticker vision. This may be useful for marketing or communication purposes but doesn't put a stake in the ground that helps everyone create measurable objectives. The more that a vision can be expressed as a visionary OKR, the one big measurable thing the whole organization is focused on, the more actionable it will be. The great nineteenth-century Prussian general and military thinker Carl von Clausewitz used the German word *schwerpunkt* to describe this feeling of collective direction. Translated as "main point" or "center of gravity," every unit in the Prussian military had its own schwerpunkt, even the support units behind the lines. In the midst of planning, or the chaos of battle, the schwerpunkt served as both a logical and emotional orientation to guide action.

STRATEGIES

Once a vision is defined, it can be broken down further into supporting strategies that provide guidance throughout the organization. Like the vision, the strategies should be clear and measurable. Using John F. Kennedy's vision of landing a man on the moon, there might have been a set of strategies to support the vision that included the science needed to accomplish the mission, keeping the astronauts alive, managing the project, and PR.

In various strategy methods, these could be called priorities, imperatives, BHAGs (big, hairy, audacious goals) or WIGs (wildly important goals). Whatever you call them, they bring everyone's attention to the choices you've made about your strategy for winning. They define what to prioritize and pay attention to during the next planning horizon. Strategies distill the vision down into a balanced set of result areas. Unlike a mission or purpose statement, which keeps us focused on one primary stakeholder group, this is where

Vision	Land a man on the moon and return him safely to the earth by the end of the decade.
Strategies	**Rocket Science** Get the vehicle from Earth to the Moon and back again.
	Life Support Keep astronauts alive and able to perform mission duties.
	Project Management Keep the project on or ahead of schedule.
	Public Relations Maintain public and bi-partisan support.

Table 4: Moonshot Strategies

we can start differentiating the value that the organization provides to different groups. It can help ensure that the strategy is balanced. In the example above, the primary customers for Life Support are the astronauts. Customers for Public Relations include the public, the news media, and the US Congress.

OKRS START AT THE TOP

The OKR process evolved in Silicon Valley, a realm of fierce competition. Consider that the bestselling book written by Andy Grove of Intel, one of the godfathers of OKRs, was titled *Only the Paranoid Survive*. The technology industry has constantly demanded the creation of products that haven't been thought of before, crossing one performance threshold after another.

This kind of thinking and creating requires the ability to focus tightly on what matters, which is expressed as purpose, values, vision, and high-level strategies. But aspiring to a goal that hasn't been reached before changes the brain. We know that we don't know how to achieve the results we've signed up for. We come up against the limits of our mental models and have no habits in our bag of tricks to fall back on. This kind of ambition is bound to feel uncomfortable.

OKRs have a simple formula. The O stands for objective and KR stands for key results. An objective is a qualitative, inspiring, actionable statement of direction. The visionary OKR expressed by President Kennedy was *Go to the Moon*. Key results are quantitative outcomes, metrics that will be used to determine if the objective has been achieved. In that case, the key results included not only reaching the moon, but returning the astronauts home safely, and achieving all this by the end of the 1960s. In honor of that historic achievement, the most ambitious OKRs are referred to as *moonshots*.

Any of the elements inside the strategy stack—vision, strategies, goals and projects—can and should be framed as OKRs. The most actionable visions have measurable key results. In the early 1990s, for instance, Starbucks' vision was "2000 in 2000," which was a commitment to open two thousand stores by the year 2000, a key result they surpassed long ago. Using the OKR format fights the tendency to write these high-level strategy elements using weasel words. At minimum, even if one is stuck with a weaselly mission and vision, the use of an OKR to describe it can defuse its power of obfuscation. This is because OKRs force us to commit to something very specific.

You could choose to believe that measuring something as grand as a vision statement somehow cheapens it, reducing something emotional and inspiring to the level of something materialistic and quantitative. But like President Kennedy's moonshot, OKRs are designed to be both inspiring and measurable. And like von Clause-witz' schwerpunkt, every unit at every level in the organization can be empowered with a vision, strategies, and goals expressed as OKRs. This brings engagement, inspiration, and confidence closer to every team and employee.

5 | COMMIT

L ET'S SAY YOU'RE IN A SAILBOAT, and you want to get to a low island that is ten miles across the ocean. You know it's there, but you can't see the island over the horizon. Because of Earth's curvature, you can only see about two and a half miles if you're sitting in the boat at sea level. If you stand up, you can still only see three miles ahead. In fact, you would need to be at the top of a sixty-foot mast in order to see the island! As you sail, your boat is subject to shifting currents and winds, and because of that, you will need to adjust the sails and tack. If a storm blows up, you may not be able to see far at all, nor would you be able to climb up a sixty-foot mast. You may need to take the sails down until it blows over. Your trajectory will not be a straight line to the island.

Thinking about this in strategic terms, your vision, your desired future state, is to get to that island. That's your focus. But because your sight is limited and you are constantly buffeted by emerging forces like the wind and the current, you will need to go up the mast, look around, and assess the situation periodically. You will then decide if you need a new tack or if you need to adjust the sails. Once you settle into it, you can hold your course for the time being. It's a short-term iteration on the way to your bigger vision.

This is a big lesson we've learned from the world of Agile. A development team meets with a customer or product owner, and it is agreed what functionality will be produced in the next two-week sprint. Then it's the job of the product owner or customer to go away and leave the team to determine how they will do their work. No second thoughts. That comes at the end of the cycle when the work is evaluated. This produces a mindset of simplicity in the midst of all the complex possibilities the team could consider. The team can relax and say, "All we need to think about is doing these three things." All the other possibilities are temporarily out of scope. We use the term *commitment* because it's an agreement to a particular outcome made by the team and its customers.

Goals set in the Commit stage are business outcomes we will achieve in the short-term to move toward the longer-term accomplishment of the vision and strategies.

Commitment is an emotional experience. It's the moment when you say, "I've made up my mind, and this is what I'm doing." It's actually a moment of relaxation and settling into the simplicity of a short-term goal that's right in front of you. You commit to one step at a time, do it, and learn from the results.

Agile strategy management combines strategy formulation with execution. In the Focus stage, vision and strategies express the formulation of strategy. The goals set in the Commit stage are about execution, what we will actually achieve, right now, to move toward accomplishment of the vision and strategies. OKRs are useful compass headings at both levels, but OKRs in this step are short-term, typically no longer than one quarter.

THE EVOLUTION OF OKRS FOR STRATEGY EXECUTION

OKRs did not simply emerge at Google somewhere around the year 2000. OKRs are the latest evolution of goal-setting practices that started in the 1950s with Peter Drucker's management by objectives (MBO).[16] These were further developed by Kaplan and Norton in the 1990s with the publication of *The Balanced Scorecard: Translating Strategy into Action*. Management by objectives recognized the need for knowledge workers (a term coined by Drucker) to act independently rather than simply follow a pre-set script. In Drucker's original vision, these objectives were to be cascaded through the organization, with each level developing its own objectives that support the objectives of the level above. Objectives had to be supported by quantitative measures so that managers could measure their actual performance against the set objectives. MBO was a model that emphasized the role of the individual manager, as opposed to the team or the organization.

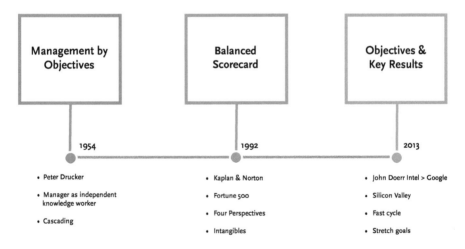

Figure 10: OKR Heritage

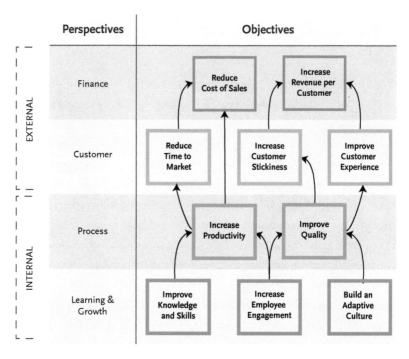

Figure 11: Balanced Scorecard Strategy Map

By contrast, the emphasis of Kaplan and Norton's balanced score-card was organizational performance, based on the study of Fortune 500 companies. This was an elegant and robust model that addressed the growing recognition of the value of intangible assets like skills, culture, and business processes. Kaplan and Norton proposed a holistic model that regarded strategic performance as a causal chain of results in four perspectives: learning and growth; internal processes; customers; and finance. The balanced scorecard became the foundation of an integrated strategy management system. It is a framework for establishing high-level strategy, creating outcome-based strategic performance measures based on clear objectives. This provides a framework to prioritize specific initiatives designed to achieve the desired outcomes.

One of the great contributions of the balanced scorecard has been the strategy map. The strategy map is a multicausal model for visualizing and communicating how achievement of an integrated set of objectives and measures will support the organization's vision. A strategy map is a simplified systems diagram that shows how investments in learning and growth and business processes—the two internal perspectives—will lead to positive business outcomes in the external perspectives of customers and finance.

When I discovered balanced scorecard in 2001, I thought I'd found the Holy Grail of management. I'd spent the early years of my career in human resources, then information technology. My frustration with the support units in which I found myself was born from never feeling that my work was truly strategic and meaningful. Mapping out the chain of causality across a strategy map using the four perspectives of Kaplan and Norton creates a holistic model of performance. The logic of the map can be tested through evidence and continuously improved. And as a communication vehicle, the strategy map and scorecard create a line of sight so employees can see how they contribute to the whole. Everyone in the organization can find an objective on the map that he or she contributes to, with specific outcome measures defining success. It's a fantastic framework for defining continuous improvements in a relatively stable environment.

After more than fifteen years of working with balanced scorecards, I began seeing some obstacles limiting the utility of this very elegant idea in practice. The typical advice has been to develop twelve to fifteen objectives with associated metrics across the four perspectives. This makes sense in large and complicated organizations looking for a comprehensive dashboard, rather like the control panel on a jetliner. But it fails to address the challenges of complexity and overwhelm, and in fact it can contribute to them. Organizations come up with more metrics than they can reasonably track, let alone make sense of in a way that supports decision making. And the process tends to generate a long list of initiatives that, more often than not, don't get done. The source of these problems is the assumption that the scorecard should comprehensively map out a three-to-five-year planning horizon. This leads participants in the planning process to include every possible action that they can imagine will help achieve the vision, because this is the only shot they will get at it for the next several years. Unfortunately, doing so means that they often start more than they should and finish less because they have created a monster Gordian Knot of projects to manage.

This all came to a head one day when I was teaching a balanced scorecard course in San José, California. The workshop included people from Intel, HP, Google, and Microsoft. The feedback I got was direct: "This is an elegant and comprehensive model, but there's no way I can take this back to my company. It's actually *too* comprehensive. It's too heavy on design up front, and too light on adaptation. We have to be more agile than that." Some participants started telling me stories about how this was done in their companies. The tables were turned, and I started learning from my students. That was the beginning of my journey to find out what it means to start less and finish more.

All good goal-setting systems combine an objective with key results, whether or not they use those exact words. We saw this in Drucker's management by objectives. It's true of the balanced scorecard. It's the same with so-called SMART (specific, measurable, achievable, relevant, and time-bound) goals. There's an objective—which is stated as a qualitative aspiration—and several key results that are concrete, measurable targets. This OKR combination is what I call the molecular unit of goal setting. The molecule behaves differently depending on the conditions it's in, though.

Think of it like a water molecule, an oxygen atom and two hydrogen atoms. Let's say the oxygen is like the objective and the hydrogen atoms are the key results. Depending on the temperature, the molecule can be locked in a rigid frozen state, can flow as a liquid, or can release into the air as a vapor. Creating a balanced scorecard with multiple objectives and results across four perspectives designed to last three to five years is like frozen water—which may make sense if there's a need for that level of stability. The OKR approach, by contrast, is like a rapidly flowing stream with a review of planning assumptions and high-level strategy every quarter that frames short-term commitments.

QUARTERLY PLANNING AT RALLY

Rally Software was a pioneer in developing agile software development tools. They practiced what they preached, constantly developing new ways to build both strategic and operational agility. The founders, Ryan Martens and Tim Miller, were well versed in agile methods for software development but wanted to apply agile principles organization-wide.

Their strategy stack started at the top with a three-to-five-year *true north* that served as a long-term vision and included several enterprise-level OKRs. This was supported by a more detailed vision and performance metrics for the fiscal year. Three measurable *mother strategies*, in turn, supported the true north. To activate the mother strategies, initiatives were developed both company-wide and within departments. Posters of the true north, the mother strategies, and their core values were displayed all over the Rally campus in Boulder.

Every quarter, company leadership held a steering meeting with all managers, inviting key clients and partners as observers. Remote managers in other cities were connected via high quality video feed and a tool that enabled real-time multi-threaded conversations.

The purpose of the meeting was to steer the next quarter's work based on the previous quarter's learnings. The meeting started with a review of the business context going into the next quarter, including assessment of the market and competition, along with performance against the current quarter's goals. This led to a discussion of what areas of performance needed to be improved. Priorities were set for the next quarter, followed by a discussion about how to maximize flow on these priorities by and between each department. In an Open Space session, anyone could identify topics, ideas, or bottlenecks. Others could flow freely from topic to topic depending on interest over the next hour. So it was a process of committing to quarterly goals as well as improvements to workflow and communications, all guided by a freshly shared understanding of the assessment and focus. Towards the end of the meeting, the visiting customers and partners were asked for their observations. Then there was a ceremony in which everyone indicated their commitment to the next quarter's plan.

THE QUARTERLY OKR CYCLE

Using the agile strategy model, the process looks like this:

REVIEW PLANNING ASSUMPTIONS

In some companies, I've seen this simply take the form of a thirty-minute report from the CEO or vice president of marketing, but there are ways to go even deeper into the organization. Everyone in the meeting is likely to have some combination of contacts with customers, competitive intelligence, and knowledge of relevant trends. The agenda should include a review of the last quarter's results and a discussion of any recent changes or disruptions in the business or industry.

Figure 12: Quarterly OKR Cycle

CONFIRM STRATEGY

Depending on how well the planning assumptions are standing up, the elements of the minimum viable strategy—vision and strategies—can be confirmed or adapted to new realities. (Any changes to purpose and values are longer-term and likely to be too time-consuming for a quarterly meeting.)

DRAFT AND ALIGN OKRs

At this point, teams begin drafting OKRs for the following quarter. One approach is to have a big-room meeting, a one-day event that starts with the company-wide meeting described above. Following that, each team drafts its OKRs, presents them to the large group, and then negotiates alignment with other teams and senior leaders.

MANAGE ACTION COMMITMENTS

Once the OKRs are approved, teams move into the weekly action cycle, developing and executing short-term action commitments.

MEASURE RESULTS

At the end of the cycle, key results are measured to see if these actions had the desired effect. This leads to dialogue about what worked, what didn't, and why. Moving into the next cycle, objectives and key results can be kept as is or modified.

GETTING READY TO CREATE OKRS

How do you come up with OKRs for your team in the first place? Before you start, review how the deliverables from the Assess and Focus steps impact your team.

PLANNING ASSUMPTIONS

There may be certain assumptions that arise from the assessment process that are relevant for a particular team. The figure below illustrates how the social media team at a wellness resort did this. One important planning assumption arose from the Assess stage. Instead of using travel agencies to book vacation trips as they had in the past, prospective guests are now going online themselves and shopping around. For that reason, building a captivating, standout website has become critical.

1. Relevant Planning Assumptions	2. Team Mission
Prospective guests have lots of options to choose from and prefer to book themselves.	We use social media to attract guests to Bodhi Beach.
3. Team Objective	**4. Key Results**
Build an awesome website that makes signing up for a week at Bodhi Beach irresistible!	20% Click-through rate Time spent on site > 2 minutes Conversion of 5% to guests

Table 5: Wellness Resort Social Media Marketing Team OKR Example

TEAM MISSION

The team needs a shared view of why they exist. Create a team-level purpose that clearly states how the team contributes to the overall organization. This is especially useful in the case of support departments like human resources, finance, facilities, or legal that don't directly provide the core service to the company's external customers. Having the conversation builds meaning and a line of sight to strategy for the participants.

CONDUCT A TEAM-LEVEL OTSW

One way to identify areas for improvement is to conduct an OTSW analysis for the team itself. Scale the OTSW down to your team. For example, your customers may be another team within the organization. What opportunities and threats within the organization are relevant to you?

DRAFTING OKRs

Once you've got a good team-level assessment and focus, here are some suggestions for generating OKRs:

CASCADE FROM THE ENTERPRISE STRATEGY

Look at the strategy of the whole organization. If strategies—or better yet, enterprise-wide OKRs—have been established, how can your team contribute to one or more of them? Sometimes these contributions are very direct. For example, if an overall sales target has been set, a regional sales team can quantify how much they will contribute. In other cases, it may be indirect. Is there something the HR department can do to better equip the sales team for success?

LOCAL BOTTLENECKS

What bottlenecks is your team facing that get in the way of productivity or quality? These become more obvious if you've done a team-level OTSW and understood the needs of your internal customers. If these bottlenecks are between you and another team, is there a way to share an OKR that addresses it?

SMALL BETS

An OKR can be a way to frame a limited bet. For instance, if you are a retail company with multiple locations, you can experiment with creating a new customer experience at one location. If it works, scale it up to other locations. If it doesn't, what can you learn?

LEARNING

Another source for OKR ideas is the list of critical uncertainties or unknowns you've identified in the assessment step. What do you wish you knew about what your customers think and what they value? Is there a way to learn more about that?

DISCIPLINED EXPERIMENTATION

Objectives and key results in a predict-and-plan environment operate under the assumption that their achievement will be beneficial and just need to be well executed. In an agile strategy environment, this is not necessarily true. You know the outcome you want, you don't necessarily know how to get there, and you must validate the best approach. You need the rapid learning cycle that OKRs can provide to understand cause and effect. Once you've validated this experimentally, you can scale up an effective solution.

Thomas Edison has been paraphrased as saying he learned a thousand ways not to make a light bulb until he found one that worked. It may be more accurate to say that the light bulb was an invention with a thousand steps, many of which Edison did not know ahead of time. He failed forward, learning every step of the way, because every failure produces data that can be used to move you forward. This is a process of disciplined experimentation. It's disciplined because it's joined to the larger vision, strategies, and outcomes, but it is experimental because in a complex environment, it just has to be.

Disciplined experimentation begins with a problem. For example, a product you sell may be losing ground against a competitor. Do you know the cause? How confident are you that you know what that cause is? It's important to surface and challenge assumptions about the cause. There may be more than one possible hypothesis about what's causing the problem. These hypotheses can generate one or more experiments, framed as OKRs. For example, Rally Software developed a clear procedure for framing and documenting experiments, using the form shown below.

The experiment name serves as the objective. The key results are the listed measures and the learning that is gained. Notice that experimenters at Rally set out to disprove, rather than prove, the hypothesis in the experiment. This was a way to cut through confirmation bias, that is, seeking information that would prove what they believed to be true already. Also, the design of the experiment requires a safety assessment and plan. Disciplined experiments are not

Experiment Name:		Team Members:
Date:	Version:	Mentor:

Background *What do you want to learn and why?*	Measures *What will you measure to invalidate your hypothesis? To indicate safety? To indicate you should amplify?*
Frame the experiment *What is the problem that inspires your experiment?*	Experiment backlog *What is the stack ranking of all actions needed?*
Hypothesis to test *Is this hypothesis falsifiable?*	Experiment results and learnings
Experiment details *How will you attempt to falsify your hypothesis?*	
Safety: *How is the experiment safe-to-run, and how will you recover?*	Next steps *Given what you learned, what's next?*

Table 6: Rally Experiment Form

intended to create undue risk for the rest of the organization. The team framing the experimental OKR must identify everything that might go wrong and have a plan in place to mitigate or recover from any damage that might occur. At Spotify, another company that has publicized how they conduct experiments, this is referred to as *limiting the blast radius.*[17]

Zachary Ross is a senior technical program manager at Google. Working in a highly matrixed organization, he supports an organization of 120 engineers, product managers, and user interface designers. There are twelve teams in this organization, and he works with them to coordinate the establishment of annual and quarterly OKRs. All of the teams have to integrate their work to deliver a single product, so shared OKRs are common.

Google has high-level strategies that change every year. For example, one year it was Mobile First. This meant that, when setting OKRs, teams needed to think about the experience of mobile users when designing applications. Every OKR did not have to align specifically to that strategy, but people writing OKRs needed to articulate why they were working on a given objective if it didn't.

This permission to set one's own goals is driven by Google's culture and the large number of millennials in the workforce. Millennials want ownership of their work and are far more motivated if they have more choice in what they work on.

Creation of OKRs happens during a two-week period that straddles the end of one quarter and the beginning of the next. Everyone is made aware of the higher-level strategies, but rather than cascading down, OKRs are initially drafted in a bottom-up fashion. It's a negotiation. Senior leaders review the OKRs and may agree or disagree. It is clear which OKRs support higher-level OKRs and which do not. Typically, 60 percent are not aligned with higher-level OKRs. After OKRs are approved and put into action, there's a mid-quarter review to ensure things are on track. That review may be more often if the OKR is especially critical.

Because these are engineering project teams, they tend to take on more OKRs per quarter than a team with operational responsibilities would, typically seven to ten. Nonetheless, they have learned not to try to use OKRs to cover everything a team does. This was a practice in the past, but it proved exhausting. OKRs describe the strategic goals for the team, but there's a lot of day-to-day work that must go on. As Zack puts it, "Everybody needs to dig a ditch once in a while."

Google uses an internally developed software application called Easy OKRs to track progress. The system transparently keeps track of all OKRs and their grades, and these are visible to everyone. It's expected that teams will achieve 60–70 percent of their OKRs. But OKRs are not used to gauge individual employee performance. At Google, it really is okay to fail. This is a deliberate cultural strategy to encourage employees to take risks. For instance, one employee put some new software into production that inadvertently caused AdWords to go down for forty-five minutes, resulting in millions of dollars in lost revenue. He was not fired. Instead, he served on a team that did a root cause analysis to understand why it happened and how to avoid it in the future.

One of the more striking things about Zack's experience at Google is the flexibility with which OKRs are applied. Not all OKRs last a quarter. Some are longer and some are shorter. They are not an Agile shop with fixed-length sprints. "We have talented people who can manage and communicate," Zack says. In other words, trust people to make commitments that make sense rather than following a fixed schedule. Problems emerge and evolve faster than ever. Teams have to be willing to throw away work that no longer promises value.[18]

OKR GUIDELINES

HOW MANY OKRs PER TEAM?

OKRs are a way to put attention on a minimal number of priorities at a time to reduce complexity and overwhelm. The number of OKRs your team takes on will depend on the team's capacity for improvement projects in addition to normal daily work. The original adopters of OKRs were engineering and marketing teams focused on specific products. Everything these kinds of teams do is part of a larger project, and each team may have up to seven OKRs at a time. These teams don't have any category of work that could be called business as usual, but most of us do.

When the team's work consists of responding to customer needs, as with health-care teams, or providing a highly transactional function like financial reporting, it's more challenging. Start with one objective to begin with the first quarter you try OKRs and build from there if you have the capacity. It's not necessary that you use OKRs to describe everything your team does. That would be a pointless and exhausting exercise. Use OKRs to prioritize and focus on the most important thing, not necessarily the most urgent.

BALANCING OBJECTIVES

One of the greatest contributions of the balanced scorecard has been the idea that strategic performance is holistic. It arises from a healthy interaction of people, business processes, technology, customer value, and financial results. It can be helpful to brainstorm OKRs in each of these perspectives and see which ones feel most urgent. An OKR for the people perspective might be reducing job stress, for example.

BALANCING KEY RESULTS

Create three to five key results for each objective. There's a good reason for this. Let's say, for example, that we have *improve hospital operations* as an objective for a clinic. If the focus is only on a key result like an improvement in labor productivity, we may be creating an undesirable and unintended consequence. Staff will figure out that they are being rated solely on their efficiency and will be discouraged from providing all the extras that comprise good patient care. So we pair productivity with a second key result, a Net Promoter Score of patient satisfaction, asking every patient if they would recommend the clinic to a friend or family member in need. Thus, staff will know that they need to consider both. Having to operate and make decisions within constraints is more meaningful than just following a script.

The example below is a case in which a third key result is needed on top of the two mentioned above, one that is a milestone. The hospital needs a plan that takes past performance and other environmental factors into account to help define other objectives and target results that will lead to future growth. Key results often have to be just milestones, especially in the beginning, with no clear measure of a business outcome. It is assumed and hoped that achieving the milestone will lead to the outcome at some point in the future. In fact, many of the key results shown in accounts of the early days of Intel and Google are clearly milestones, not outcomes.[19]

Objective	Improve hospital operations	Comments
Key Results	1. Productivity or revenue/cost ratio	*These two balance each other. Too much focus on cost reduction can degrade customer experience and vice versa.*
	2. Net Promoter Score	
	3. Completion of operational plan	*This is a "milestone" measure, generally less desirable than an "outcome" measure, but sometimes necessary in order to establish outcome measures in the first place.*

Table 7: Balancing Key Results

TIMING

When it comes to timing, the most important rule is to find a rhythm that's right for your organization or unit. Some companies create annual OKRs for the whole organization and quarterly OKRs for teams, called *dual cadence*. Fast moving organizations like startups may create a fresh company-wide OKR every quarter. If you're going to go any longer than a quarter (and even if you aren't), it's essential that you implement the weekly cadence described in the next chapter to ensure that you keep forward momentum. Another option to keep things moving is to retain the same objective for the next quarter but create new key results. For example, in a motor vehicle department, reducing customer wait time is an objective that may be a focus for years. Different key results may measure progress over time, for instance, installing a new queuing system one year and a faster photo ID system the next year.

TRANSPARENCY

One of the hallmarks of Silicon Valley OKRs is transparency. At Google, each employee's OKRs, from the top down, are actually listed next to their name in the company directory. This is a much more interesting way to find out who does what than looking at an organization chart.

We have been implying that OKRs are a mostly vertical phenomenon, with the alignment going from the top down and from the bottom up. Atticus Tysen, CIO for Intuit, tells of how he implemented OKRs in the IT function to aggressively move all Intuit products from the desktop to the cloud. He committed early to a software solution that provided complete OKR transparency to every desktop and phone, with unexpected results. Because everyone's OKRs were visible to everyone else within his organization, conversations started happening across the silos in the organization, leading to unexpected alliances and shared OKRs that accelerated the process beyond his wildest expectations.[20]

ALIGNMENT WITH HIGHER-LEVEL AND PEER OKRS

In practice, a reasonable benchmark is for 50 percent of the OKRs to align directly to a higher altitude OKR, and for 50 percent to serve specific aspirations of the team. This benchmark will vary. At Google, for example, 60 percent of OKRs come from the bottom up. OKRs can also be aligned with or even shared with peer-level teams.

COMMIT TO OUTCOMES, NOT A TO-DO LIST

Especially in the beginning, it is easier to develop OKRs that are actions or milestones. As we saw in the hospital example, completing a marketing plan might be seen as a necessary milestone. Even Google did it that way! But don't confuse that with a business outcome. Reading an objective should always remind you of why you are doing something. Why are you creating the marketing plan? Wouldn't you create a better plan if you kept in mind the larger purpose that the plan will serve? In this case, it would be more useful to reframe the objective as *improve alignment of sales to marketing strategy*. Completing the plan and communicating it to the sales team are milestone key results to help you get there, not the real objective.

The commitment you make at this stage is to measurable results that matter to a customer or some other stakeholder, not how you are going to get there. A customer can be your external customer, the buyer of your product, or a shareholder. Or they can be an internal customer, such as other employees. Outcome measures can include things like new revenue, protection of existing revenue, reduced cost, reduced risk, getting to market faster, increased employee engagement, knowledge of what customers value, and improved customer experience, value, or satisfaction.

As with every guideline, there is an exception that proves the rule. It might be necessary to get something done, something you already know how to do, just to get you to the next stage. When starting to use the OKR approach, setting key results based on milestones is a step in the right direction. It will help get teams in the habit of setting quarterly goals and tracking progress. For example, one client of mine wanted to improve employee engagement as an objective, with a key result being better employee retention in his department. But he didn't know how to do that yet. His first OKR was simple. He would meet with all fifty-five employees in his department to understand how they felt about their jobs. It was an assessment and learning OKR for him. This baseline of information helped him create an OKR for the following quarter to identify actions he could undertake to improve engagement. He believed better engagement would reduce turnover. He knew he had a longer-term objective to improve employee retention, but he didn't expect to see those results until the end of the first year.

OKRs are the engine of strategic agility.

Creating, implementing, and learning from OKRs every quarter is the engine that will build strategic agility throughout your organization. OKRs can be used to align teams with organizational strategy, solve workflow problems between teams, and learn more about what your customers value. By creating an iterative, team-level goal-setting process, OKRs build greater employee engagement and tap the collective intelligence of your workforce. The best OKRs focus on business outcomes: impacts on employee engagement, productivity, customer value, and financial performance. In an agile approach, teams commit to improving outcomes but maximize flexibility about how to attain them.

6 | ACT

TEAM GOALS, AS DESCRIBED IN THE LAST CHAPTER, are commitments to measurable business outcomes, not the projects or activities that take you there. That's why we make a distinction between the Commit step and the Act step. But Act is where the rubber meets the road. Without defining and executing activities, you'll never get to the outcome.

Rather than identifying the precise actions that are needed to achieve strategic goals ahead of time, agile organizations iterate as they go along. For that reason, the Act step draws heavily on project management techniques that have been developed in the Agile software world. The most important guideline is to minimize the number of to-do items you have on your plate at a given time. Agile people call this *minimizing work in progress*, and this is the cardinal rule of workflow management. It's the key to starting less and finishing more on a day-to-day basis.

FLOW

In the agile mindset, time and attention are recognized as the scarcest resources we have. Agile organizations build the capacity for fast, high-quality workflow that minimizes wasted time and confusion.

In an agile mindset, time and attention are the scarcest resources we have.

Many organizations get this all wrong. They track individual utilization—how busy an individual is—as a way to measure productivity. The fact is, most work is accomplished by teams, often in a value chain that involves other teams. It's better to measure flow: how fast value is created for a customer at the end of that value chain.

Psychologist Mihaly Csikszentmihalyi has spent a career studying flow. He defines flow as a state of energized focus that enables high performance under conditions of complexity.[21] It's what athletes call *being in the zone*. Flow isn't a big mystery, it's something we've all experienced. Maybe you've had the experience of being on a good sports team or in a band where there was just the right combination of challenge, discipline, and playfulness at the same time.

Flow is enabled on a team when the following conditions are present:

- CLEAR OBJECTIVES: The activity must have a clear set of goals and standards of success. OKRs provide this.

- TRUST: Communication is open and constructive. Diverse ideas are welcome. Clear commitments are made. Interpersonal feedback is freely offered and received, and problems are dealt with quickly.

- AGENCY: The team and the individual have a bias for action. They are clear about the bounds of their authority to decide and act and are given as much authority as possible.

- MINIMAL DISTRACTIONS: Intense and focused concentration on the present moment is essential for complex tasks. Minimizing work in progress enables this.

- IMMEDIATE FEEDBACK: The progress of work is transparently evident. This is reinforced with visual displays of progress and face-to-face communication. *Information radiators* (think of a scoreboard) serve as a single source of truth.

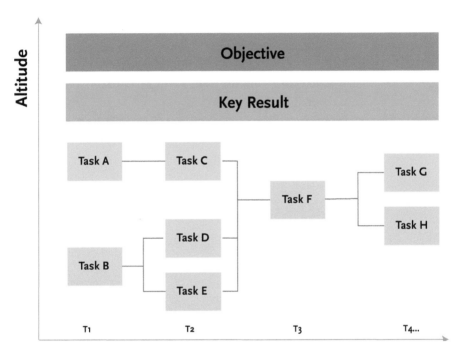

Figure 13: Define Objectives and Key Results First, Then Projects

MAKING AND MANAGING ACTION COMMITMENTS

Once OKRs are agreed to for a quarter, teams move into a regular weekly cycle of action commitments to do what it takes to achieve the key results. Without having regular conversations about the status of your OKRs, the tendency is to "set it and forget it."

People tend to be much better at making commitments than actually achieving them. Let's unpack what goes into a healthy commitment and understand where things go off the rails. Action commitments are promises made from one person to another, or to the team as a whole, to get a specific task done. For a commitment to be meaningful, it must be based on three things:

- Agreement within the team about what needs to be accomplished as a group.
- Someone requesting help with a task or offering to help someone else. The offerer is the supplier of the work, and the requester is the customer.
- A clear *definition of done*, the conditions that will satisfy the customer.

Saying "yes" is meaningless unless we have the power to say "no."

For this to be a healthy commitment, the supplier of the work must not only understand what needs to be done but also have the skills to do the work and access to necessary resources. These resources might be help from others, access to tools and technology, or the time to get the job done. And they must be sincere in their intention. We live in a culture of over-commitment. It often feels easier to say yes even if we doubt we can get the job done, or worse yet, don't really intend to do it but just want to get out of the meeting. And saying "yes" is meaningless unless we have the power to say "no." Sometimes the supplier may feel they have no choice but to agree due to power dynamics. To have skill in making healthy commitments, it's essential to be able to say no when someone asks for help or makes a request.

Once an action commitment is made and work is underway, often some kind of obstacle emerges. We might not feel as clear as we thought about what we agreed to do, we might realize we don't have the skills to do the job, or some resource we counted on is not available. We might just make a mistake. We might simply be falling behind due to other issues. On teams with a high level of trust, these issues can surface and be dealt with quickly without blame or recrimination. One of the great contributions of Silicon Valley culture is the idea that it's okay to fail—as long as something is learned.

On a high-trust team, it's okay to acknowledge being off-course and ask for help. If we've failed to follow through on an action commitment, we need to apologize and renegotiate a new deliverable or deadline. The customer of the transaction also has a responsibility to provide honest feedback. Have you ever been dissatisfied with something you've gotten from another person and not said anything? Healthy teams provide the safety to openly and formally discuss what worked and didn't work after a task or project is completed. This kind of vulnerability is essential for real learning to take place and for building trust.

CORE AGILE PRINCIPLES

Agile practitioners in the software field pioneered many of the principles we've talked about here: building strong team relationships, maximizing flow, and building in frequent feedback. Many are based on the start less, finish more principle. The principles below are described in a nontechnical way and can be adopted by any team.

MINIMUM VIABLE PRODUCT

A minimum viable product (MVP) contains the smallest set of features that provide value for a customer and in turn provide the development team with the most learning. This reduces the risk that a product will be built that doesn't address what the customer needs and wants. It also recognizes that customers don't always know what they want until they see it and can react.

SMALL BATCHES OF WORK

Big problems or initiatives need to be broken down into small batches of work. A minimum number of tasks should be in progress at once to reduce time lost to multitasking. Small batches of work can provide customer value faster than big ones and generate faster feedback for course correction. This reduces the risk that your assumptions about what customers want may be incorrect.

SPRINTS

Sprints are short intervals, typically two weeks, in which a small batch of product functionality is planned, developed, tested, and made ready to be put into production. The emphasis is on creating pieces of working product and delivering value to the customer as quickly as possible.

CUSTOMER FOCUS

Each team is in conversation with a product owner who represents the voice of the customer. The product owner negotiates features to be developed in the next sprint with the team. Then they go away and let the team determine how to get the work done on their own. At the end of the sprint, the team provides a demonstration of the working software to the product owner, who is responsible for approving it.

PERSISTENT, CROSS-FUNCTIONAL TEAMS

Work is performed by collaborative teams, not individuals. Agile teams measure productivity based on the velocity of workflow through the team rather than individual utilization. Teams used to working together, with clear authority to get the job done, can greatly reduce communication errors and the time it takes to make decisions. This is reinforced by making the team cross-functional. In a software context, this might include data analysts, coders, testers, and production specialists who can collectively create working software without handoffs to another team. The ideal team size is seven, plus or minus two people.

DISTRIBUTED LEADERSHIP

On an agile team, there is no single leader with accountability for everything the team does. The product owner plays the lead role in defining priorities for the team. But the organization of the work itself is facilitated by a scrum master who is a working member of the team and who serves as a buffer between the team and anybody or anything that could serve as a distraction. The role of the more senior managers in the organization evolves into being a coach and enabler or a higher-level product owner.

TRANSPARENCY

Open sharing of objectives, desired results, and progress updates within and across teams improves communication and innovation. Agile teams commonly use publicly visible Kanban boards to display work status. The Kanban board clearly shows which tasks are prioritized in a backlog, which are in progress, and which have been completed.

PRIORITIZATION

Time is treated as a scarce and highly valuable resource. In a highly competitive environment, delays in introducing new products or services cause irrecoverable losses of revenue and prolong other risks. When prioritizing work to be done, product owners begin by estimating the cost of delay. This includes business impacts, time criticality, and risk mitigation. They next look at the size of the work. Size includes duration, cost, and complexity. If the cost of delay for two jobs is equal, they do the shortest job first. If the size is equal, they do the task with the highest cost of delay first.

ELIMINATING WASTE

Reducing waste, and the costs that result from it, has been adopted from the lean practices that transformed Japanese manufacturing. In the realm of knowledge work, waste can include waiting, rework due to unclear requirements, unnecessary steps in decision making, stress on people due to confusion and overwork, and unused employee creativity. These are addressed by empowering teams to make more decisions on their own and optimizing the flow, or cadence, of conversations throughout the organization.

CADENCE

Information flows efficiently up and down through the organization in a regular rhythm of ceremonies. Ceremonies are structured conversations designed for efficient information exchange and idea generation, and often, as the name implies, they have an element of ritual. These ceremonies coordinate the work of multiple agile teams and tie software development into larger enterprise priorities, a process that lean practitioners call *catchball*. Someone from each team participates in meetings at the next level up, providing a link for a two-way flow of information.

The regularity of the rhythm creates a pace that enables individuals and teams to focus on their work with a minimum of external distraction, knowing that critical questions will be answered in a timely fashion.

TEAM CEREMONIES

Team ceremonies apply the concept of small batch sizes to meetings. Short, regularly scheduled meetings with a clear agenda maximize coordination and feedback and keep the team from getting off track. When meetings are held irregularly, too many agenda items pile up to deal with, and it becomes difficult to schedule everyone. Worse, these conversations can seem like an extra burden that keeps people from doing their "real" job.

Team ceremonies during an OKR cycle include two levels of check-in conversations: weekly and daily. The weekly meeting is for planning. Tasks are identified, prioritized, and assigned to individuals.

The daily check-in is a brief follow-up meeting limited to fifteen minutes. The brevity of the meeting is reinforced by a requirement that everyone meet while standing up. This is why the meeting is actually referred to as the daily stand-up meeting. The focus is on task accomplishment. The daily check-in or stand-up is not the place to solve problems. If someone is stuck, a quick decision is made about who needs to be involved in a solution. Those people then have a separate meeting to find a way to fix the problem.

COMMITMENT-BASED MANAGEMENT AT POLECAT

Polecat is a highly successful ten-year-old company of fifty employees that offers Global 500 companies real-time risk intelligence. They turn social media noise—in literally every language on the web—into meaningful information about their clients' reputations. This service enables clients to spot risks and opportunities early on and address them.

Vice President and Chief Analyst Eric Loewe leads a team staffed by analysts skilled in the unique art and science of digital listening. Tailoring their software platform, called MeaningMine, for each client, the team uses the software (which sifts through up to twenty million postings a day) to quickly find the digital risk and reputation related intelligence their clients are searching for.

Speed-to-insight is one of their product's key features. Eric says, "Speed-to-insight is one of the unique selling points of our platform. We can generate really precise, triangulated risk and reputation intelligence in a matter of weeks, something that our customers want. They're tired of paying for software that takes months to deploy. They want to start getting meaningful results in a couple of weeks, which drives how agile we as a company need to be, from sales and marketing to development to services to HR."

Polecat can offer agile intelligence because they themselves are agile. They deliver incrementally and rapidly, and they iterate together with the customer. Team members are constantly on Skype across six cities in four different time zones, addressing whatever they need to in the moment. Rather than having work flowing up and down a hierarchy, projects are based on lateral commitments negotiated between the doer of the work and the customer of the work, whether internal or external.

Eric has built a delivery organization where workflow is fluid with extremely high velocity. Work can seamlessly flow from one member of the team to another to take advantage of unique skill sets, time zones, or availability. The challenge is to take full advantage of people's capacity without overworking anyone. In network delivery, everyone is a node. If one is overloaded, it flows over to another one, much like the structure of the internet itself. This has allowed them to scale without throwing a lot of people at a given problem, keeping the company lean.

"What we do is Agile on steroids," Eric says. "As things get more complex, you can make the rules more complex or simpler. If you can simplify the rules, let people do what they do, they tend to produce twice as much, yet with more creative freedom. It's based on trust, knowing how to ask for help and get help."

This approach gives everyone a chance to learn and work on something new all the time, which in turn helps build on the collective learnings and expertise of the entire group, which enables them to deliver even more efficiently.

At Polecat, work is not seen as a set of structured tasks but rather an agreement between individuals in a network. The underpinning of this in their organizational culture is commitment-based management. One of Eric's previous jobs was with a company that offered a software platform for managing peer commitments across an enterprise, and he brought that practice to Polecat. Everyone is accountable and committed to their work. Polecat's values are principles about how to make and manage commitments, so everyone trusts their fellow colleagues to reliably deliver on time, every time. "Our team's highly communicative and collaborative culture also makes it a very fun place to work, with little turnover," Eric says. The Polecat approach has proven to be not just efficient and effective but also good for people.[22]

THE MULTITASKING MYTH

The idea that humans are capable of multitasking is one of the great myths of our age. Our brains can only focus on one thing at a time. When we think we are multitasking, we are actually doing what neuropsychologists call task switching—and doing it very quickly.

Research shows that we can refocus our attention in as little as one-tenth of a second. But what happens when we do this all day? One widely cited study showed that chronic multitasking can result in a 40 percent loss of productivity,[23] one-tenth of a second at a time. So it takes more time to complete a set of tasks if you switch between them than if you do them one at a time, and you are more prone to errors.

This is even more true for complex tasks. In fact, given a sufficient level of task switching, we become incapable of deep sustained thinking. The constant refocusing of attention is actually addictive. One researcher characterized heavy media multitaskers as "suckers for irrelevancy."[24]

Given all this, what is the advice from scientists? Simply to focus on the 20 percent of your tasks that are most important and do them one at a time, undertaking the most important tasks first. Keep in mind that excessive busy-ness gets in the way of creative thinking. Give up on the idea of efficiency when you're learning or performing complex tasks. You need time every day when you are not using your brain. These are the times when the prefrontal cortex is able to integrate information and solve problems.[25]

In addition to minimizing the number of tasks in progress at a given time, agile teams make each batch of work as small as possible. If we look at each piece of work as having a supplier, a customer, and a definition of done, we can see that this serves two purposes. First, it provides the supplier with a clearer focus and the satisfaction of getting work done regularly. Second, it reduces the risk that the product is not quite what the customer wanted or realized they needed. The longer the customer waits for a product, the more energy is wasted if it doesn't fit the bill.

To maximize flow, agile teams break projects down into the smallest increments that can deliver value. At the same time, following the agile decision making process, it would be a mistake to define every task in detail up front. Instead, start with *epics*. Rather than a specific project or task, an epic is a broad portfolio of actions designed to support an OKR. In the weekly meetings, smaller tasks are "calved off" an epic, much like icebergs off a glacier.

In the last chapter, we saw how the social media team at a wellness resort developed an OKR for the quarter. What happened after that? At the beginning of the quarter, they created three epics, shown in the table below. Each member of the team took on a specific task, with a clear definition of done, for the first week. They picked the task because that appeared to be the most logical place to start, given what they already knew and their understanding of what they needed to learn and do. At the end of the week, they each presented their work to the rest of the team and celebrated what they had gotten done.

1. Objective	2. Key Results
Build an awesome website that makes signing up for a week at Bodhi Beach irresistible!	• 20% click-through rate • Time spent on site > 2 minutes • Conversion of 5% to guests

3. Epics	4. This Week's Tasks
Understand current user behavior.	**José** • Analyze which pages have best and worst click-through rates. • Analyze how long visitors stay on each page.
Develop new graphics and photos.	**Brian** • Meet with marketing department to review current stock of photos.
Create new web architecture.	**Irma** • Identify top three platforms for speed and flexibility. • Prepare formal recommendation.

Table 8: Social Media Team OKR, Epics and Tasks

Sometimes there was a misunderstanding about the definition of "done." For example, José came in and announced that each visitor spends an average of twenty seconds on each page they visit. But that's not what Jorge, the team leader, wanted. He wanted to know which pages visitors stayed on the longest, and he wanted to see an average and standard deviation for each of those pages, not an average for all pages.

The following Monday morning, they gathered again and iden-

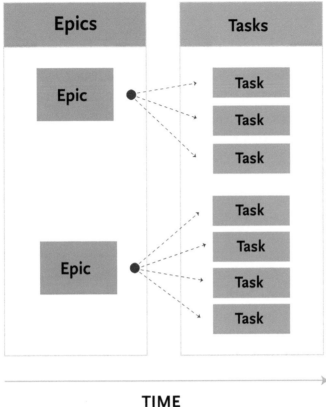

TIME

Figure 14: Progressive Refinement of Epics and Tasks

tified tasks and commitments for the new week for each epic. Based on the previous week's misunderstanding, Jorge and José got better at making a clear agreement as to what was needed, a definition of done.

Also, as the quarter progressed, some of the epics were completed and new ones were developed. These first epics mostly involved research. Decisions were made, and new epics were developed that covered the actual work of building and testing the website.

KANBAN

Kanban was a system originally developed in Japanese manufacturing and later adapted to writing software. But in fact, Kanban can be used to organize any kind of knowledge work, including web design, marketing campaigns, or personnel recruitment. Kanban is an *information radiator* that makes workflow visible, providing a single source of truth for status information and a common reference point for problem solving.

Start less and finish more by determining the most important 20 percent of your tasks. Then do them, and finish them, one at a time.

The Kanban board is a great way to organize epics and tasks and visualize the flow of work through the system. Kanban originated as a physical signboard in Japanese factories. The states of progress were columns across the top, and wooden cards were hung on nails in the appropriate column to show the status of that piece of work.

In its generic form, a Kanban board has the following columns:

- BACKLOG: work that has been defined and prioritized but not started
- IN PROGRESS: work currently underway
- COMPLETED: work that meets the definition of done and is ready for customer review
- ACCEPTED: work approved by the customer

Teams minimize work in progress by limiting how many tasks can be in that column at a time. Rather than pushing work through the system, this is a *pull* system. A new piece of work can't be pulled into work in progress until another one is finished and moved to the completed stage. Given what we know about multitasking, this is the ideal way to start less and finish more. For a team producing something for a customer, it's useful to have an *accepted* column to the right of the *completed* column. This means that the job is not done until all the requirements have been met to the best of the team's knowledge and the customer agrees that the team has met the definition of done.

Kanban makes workflow visible to everyone.

Kanbans are great tools for clarifying the intake process for any kind of work in any department. I've worked with some clients who have tension between planned work and ad hoc requests that jump the queue. One created a Kanban board with two swim lanes: one for planned work and one for last-minute requests from their manager. This way, the team was able to better communicate what other work would be bumped if they complied with an unexpected request, and they established a healthier negotiation process for unplanned work.

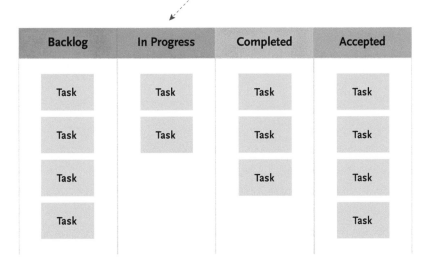

Figure 15: Kanban Board

Another column people find useful is one for blocked work, that is, when nothing more can be done due to a problem or because people are waiting for response from some other part of the chain. The volume of work in that column is very informative. If there are too many items in the blocked column and they've been there for some time, an intervention is called for. The Kanban board is a useful visual focus for a conversation about what needs to be done differently to improve flow.

Today, with people in offices across multiple time zones, there are a number of very flexible Kanban software products that can provide this transparency, track accountability, and store additional documentation. These digital Kanbans can provide electronic links all the way from the epic level down to very detailed project steps.

The use of multiple linked Kanban boards allows people to visualize work at various levels of resolution. The CEO can check in on progress on major initiatives. If there are problems or delays on one of them, she can drill down into progressively lower levels. Some Kanban tools can take you all the way down to very specific project tasks on a Gantt chart. This way, there is a clear alignment between big strategic priorities and detailed implementation that is visible to everyone.

Ethos Veterinary Health has seventeen locations across all four continental US time zones plus Hawaii. They adopted Smartsheet, an electronic work tracking productivity and collaboration tool that includes Kanban board functionality. Originally, Ethos used Smartsheet to create a Kanban board for each of their five major strategies. Specific projects for each strategy were prioritized in a backlog column and then moved through the stages to completion. Users could drill down on any project to see a more detailed project plan shown as a Gantt chart. Besides strategic projects, Ethos has discovered that Kanban can be used for many purposes.

For example, the executive team uses Kanban to identify and schedule discussion topics for weekly meetings. There's a *backlog* column. Items to be discussed that week are moved into a *confirmed topics* column. If they are not gotten to or completed, these topics can be moved to a *for next week* column. Completed items can have attached notes about discussion and decisions made. Kanban provides a powerful way to ensure that important topics don't get lost and that decisions are documented.

Ethos is growing rapidly, and they use Kanban for tracking merger and acquisition deal flow. Separate Kanbans are set up for various phases, including prospecting, due diligence, deal stage, and integration planning. Relevant electronic documents and spreadsheets can be attached directly to a card. The separate merger and acquisition related Kanbans can be rolled up into a consolidated dashboard. This has proven to be a much more accessible and easily understood single source of truth for those involved in the process.

Acting is where commitments to business outcomes are translated into specific actions by teams and individuals. Both Commit and Act, in fact, build team skills in making and managing commitments. But the time scale is different. Commitments to outcomes in the form of OKRs typically last a quarter. Action commitments are a more free-flowing, day-to-day process.

This step is about operational agility. The goals of Act are to maximize value produced by a team while minimizing waste. Waste can take many forms: waiting for decisions, confusion, and poor quality that requires rework. Strategic value for the customer has been defined by the OKRs set up in the Commit step, so in Act the team makes a priority of efficient execution.

Ensuring that value has actually been created is the next step, Learn.

7 | LEARN

THE AGILE STRATEGY MANAGEMENT CYCLE begins and ends with learning. In the world of strategic planning, the beginning is often called *assessment*. After the strategy has been implemented, there's a step at the end called *evaluation*. In fact, both of these are learning.

A few years ago, I was teaching a class in Abu Dhabi involving a planning method that used these terms. We were assigned an Arabic translator, and the first morning, he came up to me and said, "We don't have two different words for these things in Arabic. There is only one word I can use for both of these steps. What should I say?"

Interesting dilemma. How are these two words really different?

"One is what you learn at the beginning, and the other is what you learn at the end," I replied.

If you see strategy and execution as a continuous cycle, the evaluation at the end of one cycle contributes to the assessment for the next. What assumptions did the team make that proved to be true . . . or not? Were the objectives that we set three months ago achieved? If not, why not? What has been learned? What would the team do differently next time?

Here's a typical agenda for a learning conversation at the end of an OKR cycle. These questions can apply either for a team or an individual.

- What was intended?
- What actually happened?
- What is the evidence that we achieved a positive business outcome?
- If we didn't achieve it, were our assumptions incorrect?
- What did we not know when we set the OKR that we know now?
- What should we keep doing? Stop doing? Start doing? Do differently?

Learning and conversation are not separate from action. They *are* action. Learning is the way we modify the mental models we use to observe the world and make decisions. There's literally something physical happening in our brains when we do this. Neuroscientists tell us that we modify our memories every time we call them up. These mental formations are not a true picture of the world, they are at best a useful approximation. But if we continue to ground our thinking in observed experience and conversation with others, these mental formations become more useful to help us navigate the world.

Let's look at an industry going through rapid disruption and see how this works. For any kind of store selling nonperishable goods, it's become easier for consumers to shop and order products online. The losers in this battle refer to this as the *retail apocalypse*. Amazon is challenging well-established players in many verticals, including outdoor equipment. One outdoor retailer started by rethinking their definition of what a store is. What does it mean to go to the store? Is that necessarily a physical location close to home, or might it be the place the customer goes to actually recreate, using the outdoor equipment company's products? This is a profound shift in the mental model. The customer actually gets the value of the product far from the store itself. As a result, this retailer has begun framing experiments that bring their brand right to the locale where customers play, creating personalized experiences that generate revenue from lessons and equipment rental and sales. This might include offering kayaking lessons and equipment rental on the water or partnering with a ski area to take over the cross-country operation. Not all these experiments will bear fruit, but some will, based on a shift in the mental model of what a store is.

Agile strategy is a continuous learning process. We learn as individuals. A high-functioning team gets that way by learning together. And a whole organization adapts to disruption and opportunity because it learns.

DIALOGUE

Dialogue is the driver of learning and adaptation in an agile organization. It is a critical business process. As Larry Bossidy and Ram Charan put it in *Execution: The Discipline of Getting Things Done*, "Dialogue is the core of culture and the basic unit of work. How well people talk to each other absolutely determines how well the organization will function."[26]

Dialogue is a type of conversation in which the participants are open to unexpected insights and decisions. It's not like a debate, in which people tend to adopt fixed positions and defend them. A political debate consists of candidates advocating their positions and criticizing the other's positions. Dialogue demands a balance between

> *The ability to learn faster than your competitors may be the only sustainable competitive advantage.*
>
> – ARIE DE GEUS,
> *head of planning,*
> *Royal Dutch/Shell*

advocacy and inquiry. Inquiry involves asking questions to explore complex issues without knowing the answers. It requires a degree of trust, vulnerability, and open uncertainty. This creates a space in which new possibilities can emerge.

CREATING THE CONTAINER

A few years ago, I had the pleasure of being a board member of a non-profit that hosted Peter Senge, the author of *The Fifth Discipline* and a renowned organizational learning pioneer. One of the other organizers and I picked him up at the airport and drove him into town, where he was going to address a group of several hundred people in a hotel ballroom. First, we had planned to have drinks at the hotel bar with the organizing committee. As we walked into the hotel, though, Peter said, "Let's look at the room first." We walked into the ballroom to find the hotel crew setting up chairs in ranks, with an aisle down the middle and a podium set up on a platform. "This is all wrong!" said Peter. "We have to change this!" Peter wanted to set up the chairs in loosely organized pods with room to wander around them. He, I, and the crew dove in and rearranged all the chairs, ignoring the rest of the organizing committee in the bar. It was that important to him.

Once everyone was in the room, Peter refused to get up on the platform. Instead, he grabbed a mike and wandered around the room. Rather than a prepared speech, he asked questions and engaged the participants in a dialogue.

Setting the initial conditions of a conversation, including its physical shape, the setting, and the agenda, is what's called *creating the container*. Peter knew that having ranks of chairs facing an elevated speaker sets a condition, an expectation that the audience is there to listen to a person of authority, an expert. Dialogue is better conducted in a circle, where every participant is equal.

That's what might be called the physical container. Then there's a social container, in which healthy dialogue is fostered by creating a culture of safety, diversity, and trust.

SAFETY

Humans are social animals, and with a few sociopathic exceptions, most of us want to be part of a healthy, high-performing team. Yet, I believe that most of us are held back by unconscious or half-conscious social pressures, personal insecurities, and biases.

What prevents us from fully voicing what we see and what we want? The answer is usually fear. Alpha humans through history have punished dissent and rewarded loyalty and compliance. It's remarkable that this pattern is beginning to change in our workplaces. W. Edwards Deming, the American academic who became the godfather of lean manufacturing in Japan, advocated fourteen leadership principles. Number eight was this: "Drive out fear: Encourage effective two-way communication and other means to drive out fear throughout the organization so that everybody may work effectively and more productively for the company."[27] The opposite of fear is the feeling of safety, that you can "say what you see," to speak your truth to others without risking your job or your social status.

DIVERSITY

Safety is essential for many reasons, not the least of which is to foster diversity. Diversity is a powerful way to reduce bias and bring a greater variety of mental models to bear on the conversation. Diversity is often thought of only in an external, demographic way related to ethnicity, gender, or disability. But even within a relatively homogeneous group, individuals may have different thinking styles and personalities. This is called cognitive diversity. People of different sensitivities, areas of expertise, cultural origins, age, gender, and types of intelligence need to be brought together for the organization to better see things from different angles.

Cognitive diversity is a key precondition to high-quality dialogue within a company. People with different ways of thinking observe different things and observe things differently, interpreting the same information in different ways. These differences provide a rich basis for dialogue and help companies prevent groupthink and avoidance of difficult issues, the all-too typical behaviors of homogeneous teams.

An internal research effort at Google's People Analytics team, called Project Aristotle, posed the question "What makes an effective team at Google?" After determining what they meant by *effective*, the researchers gathered data from 180 teams. The number one factor, psychological safety, ranked well above all the others. Here is their definition: Psychological safety refers to an individual's perception of the consequences of taking an interpersonal risk or a belief that a team is safe for risk taking in the face of being seen as ignorant, incompetent, negative, or disruptive. In the team with high psychological safety, teammates feel safe to take risks around their team members. They feel confident that no one on the team will embarrass or punish anyone else for admitting a mistake, asking a question, or offering a new idea.[28]

TRUST

Most of us know trust, or the lack of it, when we feel it. But it's possible to define the components of trust to understand how people who work together either build trust or destroy it. Trust enables people on your team to engage with purpose, put their best ideas forward, and work together. Trust is a positive assessment of another person or group that allows us to coordinate action with them.

There are three elements of trust.

1. SINCERITY: You feel the other person understands and respects your point of view and your interests. You believe the other person does not intend to deceive you. They mean what they say and say what they mean. Another way to put this is that they are authentic.

2. COMPETENCE: You believe the other person has the ability, skill, and/or resources to achieve what he or she promises to do. The lack of one or all of these three things can cause a surprising number of broken promises. The person who has broken the promise may say "But I meant well!" in all sincerity. But this does little to help if the promiser doesn't have the skills or resources to do the job.

3. RELIABILITY: The other person has a track record of fulfilling promises over a period of time. You don't need to spend a lot of time making sure they understand your request or that you understand their promise because you've developed a shared context in which these things are easily understood.

GIVING AND RECEIVING FEEDBACK

Besides dialogue and creating a container, feedback is key to learning. Our capacity to give and receive feedback and learn from both is what makes failure worth the pain. It helps us avoid making the same mistakes over and over again. In recent years, there has been a movement from seeing the manager as teller-of-what-to-do to manager-as-coach. An important coaching role involves providing feedback. The NeuroLeadership Institute is a research and think tank that has played a big role in this movement. Do you tense up if someone comes up to you and says, "Can I give you some feedback?" Most of us do. One very useful research finding of the Institute is that offering feedback causes measurable stress in the recipient. We may be accustomed to lots of feedback early in life, but once we're adults, it threatens our sense of autonomy.[29]

As it turns out, it's also quite stressful to be asked to provide feedback. Most of us feel we lack the skills and fortitude to offer anything that is not positive. Yet, building real trust means being willing to offer a realistic assessment of another's competencies. So the recommendation is to build a culture based on individuals *asking* for feedback from others rather than offering it. In this way, both sides feel less threatened. You can get feedback more quickly and regularly, you can ask a number of people, thus reducing bias, and you can get the specific feedback you feel you need to do a better job.

Asking for feedback is a statement of openness and vulnerability. It has to start from the top. It has to be reinforced as something that top performers do to keep getting better. It needs to be modeled by leadership and supported by training to show people clearly what this kind of behavior looks like. Several OKR software vendors are building feedback tracking features directly into their systems.

OKRs AND INDIVIDUAL PERFORMANCE MANAGEMENT

The traditional approach to individual performance management is based on evaluating past performance. It often draws a line directly from performance appraisal to one's paycheck. While the need to evaluate a person's competence and ability to get things done will never go away, the emphasis is shifting. In the agile approach, the focus is on developing talent by facilitating learning.

My first job out of business school was to help create what was, at the time, a state of the art performance appraisal system. It was based on the use of behaviorally anchored rating scales, or BARS. A professor I had worked for had designed the system, and his client, a hospital with more than two thousand employees, hired me to implement it.

We broke every job down into its component behaviors. For example, a secretary's job might consist of behaviors that included reception, filing, and typing. We met with incumbents of every job to identify examples of poor, average, and excellent behavior, and we put them on a numerical scale from one to five. An example of poor performance in a secretary's receptionist function might have been "Answers phone curtly and leaves callers on hold for lengthy periods." We did have lots of fun talking through the examples, especially the bad ones. Each job could have a different weighting of the behavioral components. For example, one secretary's job might involve 50 percent reception, 10 percent filing, and 40 percent typing. Another might have a different weighting. In total, there might be one hundred jobs that involved reception, but each could be weighted differently and might include other behaviors as well.

I built a computerized application to track all the behaviors, all the jobs, and the relative weighting for each employee. It cranked out printed forms, customized for each employee, on which their performance could be documented. As a young, technically minded person, this had great appeal for me. It was as if we had modeled the entire work of the organization. Seeing the composite scores on particular behaviors could tell us where we needed to provide training or hire for those skills. It supported a less biased approach to compensation management. It was a perfect Industrial Age model, breaking the job into a set of standardized and (at least theoretically) interchangeable behaviors. These were all positive developments compared to what had gone before. But this approach achieved a greater degree of objectivity by depersonalizing the job. It was based on an unexamined assumption that the performance of any team or department in the hospital could be evaluated simply as the sum of its parts. It was a perfect example of what I've called a multicausal system. It assumed that we were smart enough to understand all the moving parts of a hospital's complicated machine and could optimize the whole organization given enough data.

What did we miss? We didn't understand that in a health-care setting, patient care is delivered by teams, not individuals. We locked employees into a predefined, rigid definition of roles and behaviors that ignored, if not discouraged, any innovative behavior or learning in response to emerging circumstances. We didn't look at performance from the standpoint of patient experience and clinical outcomes. And to keep the system up to date, we created an administrative nightmare for our own human resource department.

The traditional approach to performance management is based on a backward-facing annual appraisal process. The appraisal is meant to evaluate the past year's performance and translate that into financial rewards or punishments. For most employees and their managers, this is a time-consuming and painful process. And it is completely counterproductive in industries that must compete for talent. Donna Morris, Executive Vice President for Customer and Employee Experience at Adobe, calculated that managers there were spending an average of eight hours per employee, per year, on this process while, in her words, "demoralizing everybody." She replaced annual performance reviews with quarterly OKRs for individual employees and decoupled them from compensation.[30]

Major corporations, including Deloitte, Accenture, IBM, PwC, Gap, General Electric, Cargill, ConAgra, Intel, Medtronic, and Microsoft are following this trend of eliminating annual employee performance appraisals. Rather than a backward, once-a-year appraisal that directly impacts the paycheck, the emphasis is on frequent, forward-looking conversations. This is called *continuous performance management*.

Managers are evolving into more of a coaching role. They help teams and individuals set OKRs that align with the rest of the organization and provide a process for frequent check-ins. The emphasis is on what people are learning and how they are focusing their effort, helping to build future performance rather than simply judging the past. At Adobe, for example, managers have regular conversations with teams and individual employees to set priorities and expectations based on higher-level OKRs. There is an ongoing process of feedback and dialogue, without formal documentation. These conversations must happen at least quarterly, with encouragement to provide feedback more frequently. The human resources department has evolved from an enforcer of paperwork compliance to an enabler of constructive conversations.

The process for setting an individual OKR is more or less the same as for a team OKR. Individual OKRs can be focused on learning new skills, working out process bottlenecks with others, or contributing to higher-level OKRs. The only caveat is that for an individual, it becomes more difficult to link key results to business outcomes. Most business outcomes are driven by teamwork, not individual effort. Because of this, individual key results often need to reflect the accomplishment of action commitments, learning, or improvements to processes and relationships, rather than business outcomes.

Making the transition from a backward-looking to a forward-looking process reduces stress for both the manager and the employee. The defensiveness that comes from judging, and feeling judged, is reduced in favor of a future-oriented conversation that opens the door to inquiry, engagement, and learning.

LEARNING AND EMPLOYEE ENGAGEMENT

We are in a crisis of worker buy-in and commitment. Gallup's 2017 "State of the American Workplace," based on their database of nearly 200,000 employees, shows that only 33 percent of American workers are engaged at work. Using their well-validated Q12 survey, they found that at the other end of the spectrum, 16 percent are actively disengaged and miserable, and the remaining 51 percent are just . . . there. The same percentage, just over half, are looking for new jobs. Only one in five say their performance is managed in a way that motivates them to do outstanding work.

Only 22 percent strongly agree that leadership has a clear direction for that organization. Even fewer, 13 percent strongly agree that leadership communicates effectively with them. Why do so many employees know so little about the goals of their company?[31]

Strong employee engagement is not just a nice-to-have factor. Denison Consulting, one of our assessment partners, has shown that the cultural element that most influences financial performance is employee involvement.[32] Gallup found that business units scoring in the top quartile on engagement increase productivity by 21 percent, increase profitability by 22 percent, reduce defects by 41 percent, and reduce absenteeism by 37 percent. Will active team participation in setting and managing OKRs make people feel more engaged in their work? The rapid goal-setting and feedback cycle that OKRs create builds team members' sense of agency. Fast, useful feedback helps people learn to see how their actions cause consequences. This perception changes our behavior. With a greater sense of agency, people feel more engaged and willing to take more responsibility for the whole.

Learning helps us overcome old mental models that no longer fit the world we live in. It's the completion of a cycle that begins when we acknowledge the reality of uncertainty and seek to know more about the internal and external environment, which we've called assessment. It ends with consolidation of new information into a new mental model, a continuous process that is never truly complete.

In truth, learning is the only sustainable source of competitive advantage in a world of disruption and complexity. Learning builds the foundation for the next cycle by sharpening our assessments and helping us create more powerful strategies.

8 | BUILDING THE
AGILE STRATEGY
MANAGEMENT CYCLE

A FEW YEARS BACK, I TOOK UP CYCLING, having not ridden a bicycle since I was in junior high school. My athletic wife taught me a principle I had never heard of back when I was riding my three-speed Schwinn Tiger to school. It's called cadence. A modern bike is designed with ten or more gears that allow the cyclist to maintain a regular pedaling pace, say fifty strokes a minute. With a good bicycle that fits the kind of terrain you like to be on, you can go up the steepest hill or cruise down fast while keeping a consistent rhythm. This is great for the heart and lungs, and it allows you to travel much longer distances without exhaustion.

Cadence is a very important concept in the world of agility. The pace of work is not sustainable when it alternates between confusion over what to do next and over-the-top heroic efforts to get the job done. It is either frustrating and boring in the first case or exhausting in the second. And neither contributes to good flow, performance, or morale. Instead of imagining work as a series of disparate tasks

Cadence is a rhythm of conversations that links top level strategy with day-to-day action.

_____

or projects, the team is focused on a simple set of outcomes, and they're given the freedom to self-organize to achieve that outcome. With good cadence, the team gathers data on how much they are able to get accomplished in a given cycle, which helps them get better and better at estimating what they will get done in the next cycle.

Building strategic agility is not easy. Predict-and-plan strategies are much easier to develop. The only problem is that we now live in a world where that approach no longer works well. Strategic agility requires that you do a number of things:

- Keep a radical focus on customer value.
- Build strategic thinking muscles throughout the organization.
- Orient to a clear set of business outcomes.
- Foster healthy dialogue.
- Create a fast cycle of experimentation, feedback, and learning.

You can't achieve this by issuing orders and expecting them to cascade down through every level in the organization. Agility requires enabling the flow of ideas and information in all directions: top, down, and sideways. This flow has a cadence, a rhythm of conversations that links high-altitude assessment, vision, and strategies with day-to-day action. The exact rhythm will be different for every organization. Generally speaking, you can visualize day-to-day work nested within a longer cycle of short-term goal setting, whether planning out tasks for a particular week or setting OKRs for a quarter. The quarterly OKRs fit into a cycle of annual planning and budgeting that is longer still, within an even lengthier cycle of long-range strategic thinking that could last

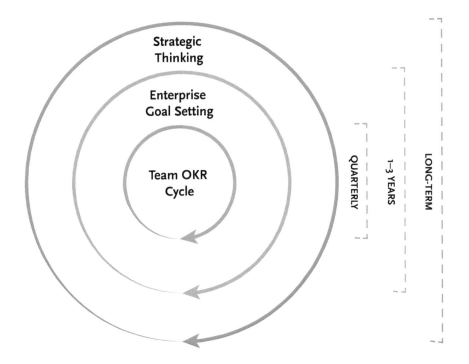

Figure 16: The Agile Strategy Cadence

three years or more. Teams at all levels learn to uncover assumptions quickly, make and manage commitments, test new ideas, build trust, and learn continuously.

Strategic thinking sessions generate new assessments of the environment, new visions, and strategies. These deep dives take time and preparation, and they generally happen annually or less often. But that frequency can and must change very suddenly in reaction to unanticipated disruption or opportunity. At the very least, key assumptions should be reviewed and questioned quarterly in competitive industries.

Enterprise goal-setting meetings use the OKR formula to set goals for the enterprise that support the key strategies. They usually follow a very regular cycle, typically for a year.

The team OKR cycle is typically quarterly, but more or less frequent depending on the operational tempo of the team. That frequency may vary between teams in the same organization.

OKR MATURITY

The perfect is the enemy of the good, as the saying goes. While I have set out a toolkit for building strategic agility using OKRs, don't expect to achieve perfection overnight, or even in the first several quarters you try it. Building alignment with enterprise strategy and getting people educated and engaged in the process takes time.

William of Ockham was a medieval English friar who formulated the idea we now call Occam's razor. There are various versions of this principle, but my favorite is *"Non sunt multiplicanda entia sine necessitate,"* which essentially means "Don't make things more complicated than they need to be." In other words, the simplest possible solution is the most useful. The word *elegant* is often used to represent this. An elegant solution is the simplest way that works to address a problem.

Start simple and build from there. You can expect to go through several levels of maturity on the way.

LEVEL ONE

Just getting people to set goals, follow through with action, and report on the outcome can be a big step. This is especially true in organizations with a high volume of day-to-day, business as usual activities, like a hospital or a finance department. Start with one OKR. It's okay if it's not a great, aspirational moonshot. It might be a *roofshot—*

something achievable that will build confidence. It doesn't have to be a big breakthrough. It might just be making some predictable process a little faster or better or learning something new about your customer. In the beginning, many people have difficulty creating business outcome measures, so just completing a project of some kind might be enough. The right outcome measures may become clear later. You're trying to build muscles for goal setting, commitment, and accountability at this stage. It may not require much deep dialogue, just getting it done. Having said that, it helps to keep pointing out the difference between activity measures (Did it get done?) and outcome measures (For what benefit?). Keep asking why the activity needs to be done, and people will start learning the difference.

LEVEL TWO

As the cycle becomes more predictable and there's been more learning about outcome measures, encourage more moonshots. Moonshots put the team into unfamiliar territory. They require more dialogue, challenging assumptions about the nature of the problem and the solution. The attitude is more experimental, validating or invalidating a hypothesis rather than simply executing a plan. The agile approach to tasks and commitments becomes more important when the team's understanding evolves week to week. Regular learning conversations are critical.

LEVEL THREE

Some of the case studies in this book, particularly the stories of Google and Polecat, illustrate what's possible after Level Two for organizations in a highly dynamic and complex environment. At Google, there's no expectation that OKRs should last exactly one quarter. Problems and opportunities emerge and evolve more quickly than that. There's an emphasis on creating commitments that make sense depending on the issue at hand and trusting people to manage those. The culture attracts and supports employees who have a self-challenging personality, so learning conversations occur frequently as needed. Polecat takes commitment-based management a step further. The cycle of setting and managing objectives is constant, supported by intense levels of dialogue. This makes sense because of the extremely agile nature of the product and the customer relationship. A small number of formal OKRs are used only to undertake improvements to internal processes and systems.

IN CONCLUSION

Whatever business you're in, surviving and thriving is an uncertain proposition. There is no permanent competitive advantage or guaranteed mandate, even for a government agency. It will not be the strongest players that survive, but the most adaptive. These are the ones who not only learn fastest but who can translate that learning into action that creates new value for customers. Building strategic agility is a goal without an endpoint, a continuous process of challenging assumptions, identifying opportunities and experimenting with new approaches.

But this is easier said than done. We live in an economy of chronic distraction. The more distracted we get and the more things we try to do as a result, the less we accomplish. We need to focus on the few things that are most important to us. Strategy is a game constrained by limited resources and competition. It requires a strong sense of purpose, vision, and values. It requires hard choices about whom we will serve, what we will provide to them, and how we will organize ourselves to do that. This economy of attention has been the central theme of this book—to start less and finish more.

The start less, finish more attitude is woven through every step of the agile strategy management process:

1. ASSESS: Simplify your environmental scan by paying most of your attention to the performance measures and trends that impact the people you most care about—your customers and a few critical stakeholders.
2. FOCUS: Create a minimum viable strategy that includes only purpose, values, vision, and a handful of key strategies, and then iterate from there.
3. COMMIT: Don't overcommit! If you're already too busy, start with one OKR per quarter and add more only when and if you're ready.
4. ACT: Identify actions in short sprints with a limit on how many tasks you have on your plate at one time.
5. LEARN: Taking the time to consolidate learning in regular team conversations will save you time in the long run by improving the quality of your decisions.

Collectively, we have created a world too complex to manage using the mindset we used to create it. Trying to resolve complexity with more complexity won't work. Like Alexander the Great hacking the Gordian Knot, complexity can only be conquered with choice, simplicity, and clarity. It's vital to understand what we truly want and value and then hold tight to that vision.

It's tempting to believe that we can get smarter and smarter because we have so much information available to us. In fact, this information glut doesn't help us cope with complexity, and it can actually make things more difficult. Our most important challenges are psychological, social, and ethical. We are creatures of habit, and our mental habits encourage us to stay in the well-worn grooves that have worked in the past.

Developing the collective muscle for strategic thinking—beginning with challenging our assumptions and mental models—is more important than ever. This is true inside our organizations. It is also true among institutions collaborating to develop new industries, regional economies, and solutions to social problems. Without the right planning and execution, though, none of this innovative thinking will bear fruit. If strategic planning feels complicated and time-consuming, if it feels disconnected from our real day-to-day work, it won't have the impact we want.

The solution is to simplify the way we think about strategy—what it is, how to develop it, and how to carry it out. Whatever lofty goals we may have, success comes down to how we focus our thinking moment to moment and how we act day to day. Starting less and finishing more is the essence of that agile mindset.

ENDNOTES

1. Shunryu Suzuki, *Zen Mind, Beginner's Mind* (New York: Weatherhill, 2001), p. 21.
2. Donald Rumsfeld, US Secretary of Defense. News briefing, February 12, 2002.
3. Author's conversation and email correspondence with Ryan Martens, cofounder of Rally Software and social entrepreneur.
4. Henry Mintzberg, *Rise and Fall of Strategic Planning* (Free Press, Kindle Edition), p. 114.
5. Gallup, 2017, "State of the American Workplace Report." Available for download at http://news.gallup.com/reports/199961/state-american-workplace-report-2017.aspx.
6. Henry Mintzberg, *Rise and Fall of Strategic Planning* (Free Press, Kindle Edition), p. 25.
7. Kenneth Olsen, Founder of Digital Equipment Corporation, in a speech to the World Future Society in Boston, 1977. In 2003, he clarified that what he was referring to was not the type of personal computer that was already on the market in 1977, but a computer that controlled every aspect of the home, such as turning lights on and off, regulating temperature, monitoring food supplies, and so

on. Ironically, with the more recent advent of the so-called Internet of Things, some of these functions are actually now becoming available. In spite of his 2003 argument that he was taken out of context, he was still proven wrong by later developments.

8. http://www.futuristspeaker.com/business-trends/turbulent-times-ahead-for-cities-63-looming-issues/.

9. Randall Rollinson and Earl Young, *Strategy in the 21ˢᵗ Century: A Practical Strategic Management Process* (Looking Glass Publishing, 2010), pp. 137–138.

10. Michael Porter, "What is Strategy?" *Harvard Business Review*, November 1996, 70.

11. There are many translations of Sun Tzu's book *The Art of War*. My favorite is *The Art of War*, Denma Translation Group (Shambhala, 2001). Drawing any modern-day conclusions while translating from ancient Chinese is fraught with peril, but this group worked extensively with Tibetan meditation master Chögyam Trungpa Rinpoche to gain insight into the ancient wisdom behind the text.

12. I am indebted to integral philosopher Steve McIntosh for his discussion of the three primary Platonic values in *Integral Consciousness* (St. Paul: Paragon House, 2007), particularly pp. 131–142.

13. http://www.wholefoodsmarket.com/mission-values/core-values.

14. Donald Sull and Kathleen Eisenhardt, "Simple Rules for a Complex World." *Harvard Business Review*, September 2012, 74.

15. These principles are documented at agilemanifesto.org

16. Peter F. Drucker, "Management by Objectives and Self-Control," in *The Essential Drucker* (Harper Business, 2001), pp. 112–126. This selection was excerpted from Drucker's original work, *The Practice of Management*, published in 1954.

17. https://labs.spotify.com/2014/03/27/spotify-engineering-culture-part-1/.

18. Author's notes, conversation with Zachary Ross, October 31, 2017.

19. See John Doerr's book, *Measure What Matters* (New York: Penguin, 2018) for examples of early OKRs in use at Intel and Google. Google has developed more emphasis on outcomes as the OKR process has become more refined over the years.

20. Author's notes, BetterWorks Goal Summit, San Francisco, April 20, 2017. See video at https://www.youtube.com/watch?v=N5Y8jyaLEvU.

21. Mihalyi Csikszentmihalyi, *Flow: The Psychology of Optimal Experience* (Harper Perennial, 1991).

22. Author's interview notes and emails with Eric Loewe, March–December 2017.

23. http://www.apa.org/research/action/multitask.aspx.

24. https://news.stanford.edu/2009/08/24/multitask-research-study-082409/.

25. https://www.psychologytoday.com/blog/brain-wise/201209/the-true-cost-multi-tasking.

26. Larry Bossidy and Ram Charan, *Execution: The Discipline of Getting Things Done* (Random House, 2011), p. 25.

27. http://www.qualityregister.co.uk/14principles.html.

28. https://rework.withgoogle.com/guides/understanding-team-effectiveness/steps/identify-dynamics-of-effective-teams/.

29. https://neuroleadership.com/.

30. For more on Adobe's approach, see http://www.adobe.com/check-in.html or Donna Morris' presentation at https://www.youtube.com/watch?v=d6rmcxS0IMg.

31. Gallup, 2017, "State of the American Workplace Report." Available for download at http://news.gallup.com/reports/199961/state-american-workplace-report-2017.aspx.

32. https://www.denisonconsulting.com/.

BIBLIOGRAPHY

Argyris, Chris. *Organizational Traps: Leadership, Culture, Organizational Design*. New York: Oxford University Press, 2010.

Bock, Laszlo. *Work Rules: Insights from Inside Google That Will Transform How You Live and Lead*. New York: Twelve, 2015.

Bossidy, Larry, and Ram Charan. *Execution: The Discipline of Getting Things Done*. New York: Crown Business, 2002.

Chaikin, Andrew. *A Man on the Moon: The Voyages of the Apollo Astronauts*. New York: Penguin, 2007.

Collins, Rod. *Wiki Management: A Revolutionary New Model for a Rapidly Changing and Collaborative World*. New York: AMACOM, 2014.

Courtney, Hugh. *20/20 Foresight: Crafting Strategy in an Uncertain World*. Boston: Harvard Business School Press, 2001.

Czikszentmihalyi, Mihalyi. *Flow: The Psychology of Optimal Experience*. New York: Harper Collins, 1990.

Denning, Stephen. *The Age of Agile: How Smart Companies Are Transforming the Way Work Gets Done*. New York: AMACOM, 2018.

Dennis, Pascal. *Getting the Right Things Done: A Leader's Guide to Planning and Execution*. Cambridge, MA: Lean Enterprise Institute, 2006.

Doerr, John. *Measure What Matters: How Google, Bono, and the Gates Foundation Rock the World with OKRs*. New York: Penguin, 2018.

Doz, Yves, and Mikko Kosonen. *Fast Strategy: How Strategic Agility Will Help You Stay Ahead of the Game*. Harlow, UK: Pearson Education, 2008.

Drucker, Peter F. *The Essential Drucker*. New York: Harper Business, 2001.

Flores, Fernando. *Conversations for Action and Collected Essays: Instilling a Culture of Commitment in Working Relationships*. CreateSpace, 2013.

Freeman, R. Edward, Jeffrey S. Harrison, Andrew C. Wicks, Bidhan L. Parmar, and Simone de Colle. *Stakeholder Theory: The State of the Art*. Cambridge, UK: Cambridge University Press, 2010.

Gardner, Dan. *Future Babble: Why Expert Predictions Are Next to Worthless, and You Can Do Better*. New York: Penguin, 2011.

Haeckel, Stephen A. *Adaptive Enterprise: Creating and Leading Sense-and-Respond Organizations*. Boston: Harvard Business School Press, 1999.

Isaacs, William. *Dialogue and the Art of Thinking Together*. New York: Doubleday, 1999.

Jackson, Thomas L. *Hoshin Kanri for the Lean Enterprise: Developing Competitive Capabilities and Managing Profit*. Boca Raton: CRC Press, 2006.

Jones, Phil. *Strategy Mapping for Learning Organizations: Building Agility into your Balanced Scorecard*. Burlington, VT: Gower Publishing, 2011.

Kaplan, Robert S., and David Norton. *The Balanced Scorecard: Translating Strategy into Action*. Boston: Harvard Business School Press, 1996.

————. *The Execution Premium: Linking Strategy to Operations for Competitive Advantage*. Boston: Harvard Business School Press, 2008.

————. *The Strategy-Focused Organization: How Balanced Scorecard Companies Thrive in the New Business Environment*. Boston: Harvard Business School Press, 2000.

————. *Strategy Maps: Converting Intangible Assets into Tangible Outcomes*. Boston: Harvard Business School Press, 2004.

Kofman, Fred. *Conscious Business: How to Build Value Through Values*. Boulder: Sounds True, 2006.

Liker, Jeffrey K. *The Toyota Way: 14 Management Principles from the World's Greatest Manufacturer*. New York: McGraw-Hill, 2004.

Mackey, John, and Rajendra Sisodia. *Conscious Capitalism: Liberating the Heroic Spirit of Business*. Boston: Harvard Business Review Press, 2013.

McChrystal, Stanley, Tantum Collins, David Silverman, and Chris Fussell. *Team of Teams: New Rules of Engagement for a Complex World*. New York: Penguin, 2015.

McIntosh, Steve. *Integral Consciousness and the Future of Evolution*. St. Paul: Paragon House, 2007.

Mintzberg, Henry. *The Rise and Fall of Strategic Planning: Reconceiving Roles for Planning, Plans, Planners*. New York: Simon & Schuster, 1994.

————. *Strategy Safari: A Guided Tour Through the Wilds of Strategic Management*. New York: Simon & Schuster, 1998.

Niven, Paul R., and Ben Lamorte. *Objectives and Key Results: Driving Focus, Alignment and Engagement with OKRs*. Hoboken: John Wiley & Sons, 2016.

Pietersen, Willie. *Reinventing Strategy: Using Strategic Learning to Create and Sustain Breakthrough Performance*. New York: Wiley, 2002.

————. *Strategic Learning: How to Be Smarter Than Your Competition and Turn Key Insights into Competitive Advantage.* Hoboken: John Wiley & Sons, 2010.

Reinertsen, Donald G. *The Principles of Product Development Flow: Second Generation Lean Product Development.* Redondo Beach, CA: Celeritas Publishing, 2009.

Ries, Eric. *The Lean Startup: How Today's Entrepreneurs Use Continuous Innovation to Create Radically Successful Businesses.* New York: Crown Business, 2011.

Rohm, Howard, David Wilsey, Gail Stout Perry, and Dan Montgomery. *The Institute Way: Simplify Strategic Planning and Management with the Balanced Scorecard.* Cary, NC: The Institute Press, 2013.

Rollinson, Randall, and Earl Young. *Strategy in the 21st Century: A Practical Strategy Management Process.* Chicago: Looking Glass Publishing, 2010.

Schmidt, Eric, and Jonathan Rosenberg. *How Google Works.* New York: Grand Central Publishing, 2014.

Senge, Peter M. *The Fifth Discipline: The Art & Practice of The Learning Organization.* New York: Doubleday, 1990.

Sinek, Simon, David Mead, and Peter Docker. *Find Your Why: A Practical Guide for Finding Purpose for You and Your Team.* New York: Penguin, 2017.

Stambouli, Christian J. *The Ukemi Way: Seven Key Practices for High Performance Project Management and Leadership in Turbulent Times.* Villa Park, CA: Blue Pueo Press, 2015.

Sull, Donald, and Kathleen Eisenhardt. *Simple Rules: How to Thrive in a Complex World.* New York: Houghton Mifflin, 2015.

Sun Tzu. *The Art of War.* Translation, essays and commentary by the Denma Translation Group. Boston: Shambhala, 2001.

Sutherland, Jeff, and J. J. Sutherland. *Scrum: The Art of Doing Twice the Work in Half the Time.* New York: Crown Business, 2014.

Suzuki, Shunryu. *Zen Mind, Beginner's Mind.* New York: Weatherhill, 2001.

Vanourek, Bob, and Gregg Vanourek. *Triple Crown Leadership: Building Excellent, Ethical, and Enduring Organizations.* New York: McGraw Hill, 2012.

Wodtke, Christina. *Radical Focus:Achieving Your Most Important Goals with Objectives and Key Results.* Cucina Media, 2016.

Worley, Christopher G., Thomas Williams, and Edward E. Lawler. *The Agility Factor: Building Adaptable Organizations for Superior Performance.* New York: Jossey-Bass, 2014.

ACKNOWLEDGMENTS

Of all the people who've helped me produce this book, two stand out. The first is my father, Reverend James W. Montgomery. An English major who taught high school and later became a man of the cloth known for his folksy sermons, he inspired in me a love and care for words. Dad would break into Shakespearean soliloquies at the dinner table, and like many of his generation, he memorized long passages of poetry in school, which he could still recite many years later. He became an author of history books and historical fiction in retirement, fulfilling a lifelong dream.

And this book could absolutely never have happened without the steady support and encouragement of Beth Marvel, my wife and business partner. Whenever I wavered, or doubted, or thought I should be doing something else, she would say, "Finish the book first." She always encouraged me to put *Start Less, Finish More* into practice.

A number of people were intellectual companions as I started thinking through how to apply agile principles to strategy. These included Gabriel Morgan, then of Microsoft, then REI, and now Starbucks; Ryan Martens, cofounder of Rally Software, and his team, including Alex Pukinskis, Jean Tabaka, and Zach Nies; and business anthropologist Marsha Shenk.

The discovery of objectives and key results was the next breakthrough. For this I am grateful to Paul Niven, Ben Lamorte, and Felipe Castro for sharing ideas and insights along the way. The connection with Paul is particularly ironic. In 1997, I was working for a software reseller in Halifax, Nova Scotia. Paul, who was working at Nova Scotia Power and developing one of the first balanced scorecards there, came to us looking for a technology solution to support it. Our software wasn't the ticket as it turned out, but the question "What's a balanced scorecard?" took me a long way.

There were a number of people who were happy and willing to talk with me and be cited as case examples. I haven't been able to fit all of them into this book. A big thank you to the informants I did use, including Eric Loewe of Polecat, Brian Cassell of Ethos Veterinary Health, Zack Ross of Google, Michael Kersten of Hill Medical Group, and Ryan Martens, cofounder of Rally Software.

A number of people reviewed various versions of the manuscript and provided useful feedback, including Beth Marvel, Marsha Shenk, Ryan Martens, Steve Denning, Chris Stambouli, Brian Cassell, David Rasch, Steve McIntosh, Rod Collins, and Bob Weil. Thank you for taking the time and care to tell me what you really thought!

Finally, I must thank the professionals who've helped me produce the book: My old friend Phil Karl, who took a chaotic pile of ideas and rendered it into the first readable version; Lora Zorian of Shambhala Publications, whose early enthusiasm and suggestions were invaluable; Megan Holstein, who designed the icons used to illustrate the agile strategy cycle; Scott Merriam, who designed the graphic figures in the book; Jeff Fuller, who designed the striking cover; Lora Zorian (again) who crafted the interior of the book; Mike Daniels for marketing and production advice; and last but surely not least, Melanie Mulhall of Dragonheart for challenging me to write my best every step of the way.

ABOUT THE AUTHOR

DAN MONTGOMERY has been training, coaching, and consulting in the areas of strategic planning, leadership development, and balanced scorecard for the past twenty years. He has taught strategy and balanced scorecard training courses in the US, Canada, and Middle East, and he has facilitated the development of strategic plans for dozens of clients. Previous careers include human resource management, counseling, software design, and information technology management.

Dan is a veteran of major consulting firms, including Accenture and Ernst & Young. Prior to founding Agile Strategies, Dan was Vice President of Professional Services for the Balanced Scorecard Institute and led the company's consulting practice. He is coauthor of *The Institute Way: Simplify Strategic Planning and Management with the Balanced Scorecard*.

Over a forty-year career, Dan has served a variety of industries, including health care, technology, human services, higher education, hospitality, natural products, utilities, government, military, financial services, social entrepreneurship, engineering, and construction. He spent sixteen of those years living and working in Canada.

In parallel with his business career, Dan has been a student of yoga and mindfulness practices since his teens. His diverse experience has informed a holistic, human-centered point of view on how culture, leadership, technology, and work process impact customer value and financial performance.

Dan is a graduate of The Evergreen State College in Olympia, Washington. He has an MBA from the University of Colorado, as well as a master's degree in Buddhist and Western Psychology from Naropa University. He serves on the Board of Directors for the Colorado Chapter of the Association for Strategic Planning.

He and his wife and partner, Beth Marvel, live in Boulder, Colorado, where Dan is an avid cyclist, golfer, and hiker.

INDEX

NOTES

NOTES

NOTES

NOTES